THE DAYS OF HEROES ARE OVER
A Brief Biography of Vice President Richard Mentor Johnson

THE DAYS OF HEROES ARE OVER

A Brief Biography of Vice President Richard Mentor Johnson

DR. DAVID PETRIELLO

Westphalia Press
An Imprint of the Policy Studies Organization
Washington, DC
2016

Westphalia Press
An imprint of Policy Studies Organization
1527 New Hampshire Ave., NW
Washington, D.C. 20036
info@ipsonet.org

ISBN-10: 1-63391-403-8
ISBN-13: 978-1-63391-403-2

Cover and interior design by Jeffrey Barnes
jbarnesbook.design

Daniel Gutierrez-Sandoval, Executive Director
PSO and Westphalia Press

Updated material and comments on this edition
can be found at the Westphalia Press website:
www.westphaliapress.org

Contents

INTRODUCTION

Over the last 200 years, the country has elected a variety of colorful figures to national office. Drunkards, racists, slave holders, philanderers, war heroes, populists, demagogues, humanitarians, misogynists, embezzlers, patriots, and nepotists, all have walked the halls of the Capitol and the White House. Yet rarely has a man been sent to Washington who could be defined by all of those descriptors at once. Richard Mentor Johnson of Kentucky was one of those men. His heroic, controversial, and eccentric life made him notorious in his day, a tragic hero who walked the stage of American politics for almost half a century.

Yet very quickly after his demise Col. Dick Johnson began to fade from public memory. Some of this can certainly be attributed to the fact that Americans tend not to immortalize Vice Presidents. After all who remembers George Dallas or Hannibal Hamlin? Many of these men have in fact emerged less well known than the failed candidates for President whom they have run against. However, even the most obscure of Vice Presidents have had numerous biographies written about them. The glaring gap in this otherwise often oversaturated market is Richard Mentor Johnson. Yet Johnson's *damnatio memoriae* seems to have less to do with his political mistakes than his personal ones. As interesting as his controversial, and in many places illegal, love life would be to the modern day public, in the nineteenth century it was downright scandalous. Portions of his own party saw it as an affront to their philosophies on the separation of the races, while conservatives saw him as a demagogue, and northern Whigs weren't quite sure whether to view him as proof of the perversions inherent in slavery or as positive step which they refused to give such a partisan Democrat credit for.

Due to this, the life of Richard Mentor Johnson, warts and all, has remained barely examined for a century and a half. Besides campaign literature from the time period and the occasional article on some quirky element of his life or career, no historian has scratched the surface of the man and made it available to the general public.[1] This work seeks to solve that gross injustice by combing through the attacks of his Whig opponents and paeans from the Democratic Party to deliver a nonpartisan biography of a forgotten American legend.

If an overall theme emerges from his life, it is that Johnson was both a true westerner and a true Democrat. As the former he was a believer in the promises and expansion of the nation; the American continent was an empire of opportunity to be wrestled into submission by daring men and women. In the latter vein he was a staunch supporter of the rights of individual against the state and a firm supporter of the idea that the national government existed to answer the needs and push forward the progress of its citizens. Richard Mentor Johnson would have been as much an animal of the Democratic Party in 2015 as he was in 1840. It is perhaps this timelessness in the American saga that should make him such a compelling and iconic figure.

Dick Johnson was a more tragic Andrew Jackson, plagued by financial issues, health concerns, the death of a wife and daughter, and the rejection of a society that he sought so hard to gain entrance to. His upbringing, valor in war, and appeal to the masses seemed to assure him of just as bright a future as Old Hickory. Yet he was a flawed doppelgänger, or more accurately a true one in the sense of the folklore that surrounds that term. He was a fetch, an identical copy of someone that foreboded doom. His ascension to the vice presidency proved to be the death knell to his career as the campaign exposed all of the flaws of the man and his performance once in office was stunted at best. Johnson was sent crashing back to Earth and despite his best efforts languished there until his death.

Yet his life was far from a failure. Johnson helped to end the practice of debt imprisonment across the nation, set up academies for the education of Native Americans, defeated (and possibly killed) one of the nation's greatest Indian enemies, staunchly supported the separation of church and state, helped to end central banking, stood up for the common man, and always sought to preserve the union. It is both these failures and successes that make him such a compelling figure to study, a fine example of a Jacksonian.

His story was far from a singularity though. The arrival of Robert Johnson, the patriarch of the family, in Kentucky in the late 1770s began the rise to power of the state's first political dynasty. All of the Johnsons proved to be notable examples of the Jacksonian ideal so evident in Richard. The story of this clan and its dominance in local, regional, and national politics from 1790 to 1850 is the story of the rise of the west, a region that was an admixture of America and the ultimate expression of democracy.

This book, while functioning as a biography of Richard Mentor Johnson, will also explore the Johnson family's unique and profound impact upon both Kentucky and the larger United States. In this sense, it will be a historical look at the rise of mass democracy in America and those who partook in it. As the republic of the elite gave way to the democracy of the many and the active, the Johnsons served as examples of this new trend. These were men who, in the words of one of Col. Johnson's eulogizers, thought it ...

> "better to stand over the open graves of all who have labored for the building up of this glorious political fabric, in the past, than blast the hopes of a world, by allowing sacrilegious hands to be laid upon the Union, to bury the hopes of freemen everywhere, by consigning to the tomb the fairest structure ever reared to protect the rights, to expand the mind, and to perfect the liberties of man."[2]

CHAPTER I

THE ARRIVAL IN KENTUCKY

" Sound the Bugles Rumpsey, Dumpsey, Colonel Johnson killed Tecumseh." The former Vice President must have chuckled to himself as he lay dying in 1850 knowing that this silly rhyme had been the thing to launch his national career. Born on a battlefield in one war, he achieved national renown on another, and used it to propel himself to the second highest post in the land. Despite the fact that he is nearly unknown today by almost all Americans, his character, personal habits, and romantic relationships were all either noteworthy or notorious during his own lifetime and afterwards. Always true to the frontier image that he sought to portray, Richard Johnson was tough, independent, and committed to the democratic ideal of the common man. And while the deaths of such luminaries as Sen. John C. Calhoun and Pres. Zachary Taylor that same year largely overshadowed his own demise, Johnson's life was as equally transformative as theirs.

A man whose life was as storied and colorful as Richard Mentor Johnson certainly must have come from an equally intriguing family. The entirety of the Johnson household in fact proved to be quite impactful on the early history of Kentucky as a state, producing legislators, generals, judges, heroes, and businessmen. The Johnsons were most likely of pure English or Anglo-Welsh stock. The Reverend John Telemachus Johnson himself, when speaking of his family's origins once said, "Robert Johnson, my father was the son of William, one of three brothers, who came from England and settled in America. They were reputed to be from Wales." While some have speculated an Anglo-Scottish or even purely Scottish background for the Johnsons, going so far as to allege that they were possibly descended from the Johnston family which held a baronetcy in Scotland since at least the time of King David II in the fourteenth century, this is doubtful.

Regardless of its royal or un-royal origins, it was already a family of minor merit through its various branches when it arrived in America a few generations prior to Richard's birth. The family could boast connections to the Cave, Suggett, Spence, Pope, and Youell clans, all of which were respected families of Old Virginia who had removed from England to seek their fortunes in the New World. On his mother's side, the future Vice President was descended from Richard Lee, a staunch royalist and supporter of King Charles I whose own ancestors boasted crusaders and various lesser nobility. Through the twisted branches of his family tree, Richard Mentor Johnson was also distantly related to Robert E. Lee, Zachary Taylor, and James Madison. If the Kentucky Johnsons were the sum of those that came before them, then they were men of bearing, martial skill, and exploring spirit.

Regardless of his origins and their genetic or economic character, the first Johnson of renown in America, William, rose to become a prominent member of old Virginia. Marrying Elizabeth Cave in 1742 he built up a prosperous plantation in Orange County on the banks of the Rapidan River. Here, William raised a family of nine children and even became a member of the House of Burgesses. Perhaps the truest sign of his status was the presence of James Madison Sr., the largest landowner in the county, as a witness to his last will and testament in 1766. His children and grandchildren would eventually populate much of the south, becoming important contributors to local and national life in their own ways.

The patriarch of the Kentucky branch of the Johnson family was Robert, who was born on July 17, 1745, in Orange County, Virginia. He grew up in the tumultuous years leading up to the American Revolution, a conflict that was to profoundly affect his life. Robert Johnson was already a wealthy man by the age of 21, having inherited all of his father's lands in Culpeper County, modern day Culpeper, Madison, and Rappahannock Counties. In 1770, at the age of 25, Robert married Jemima Suggett, daughter of James Suggett and Jemima Spence and eight years his junior. The marriage would be a fruitful one, producing at least 11 children, including Elizabeth (b.1772), James (b.1774), William Judah (b.1775), Sarah (b.1778), Richard Mentor (b.1780), Benjamin (b.1784), Robert (b.1786), John Telemachus (b.1788), Joel (b.1790), George Ward (b.1792), and Henry (b.1794).

The elder Colonel Johnson is credited in family histories with having fought at various points during the American Revolution, though much of this may be hearsay or later extrapolation. He most likely served in the militia in Orange County during the early part of the conflict, but took part in no major battles or campaigns. By the autumn of 1779, he was transporting his growing family westward from the frontlines of the war with his brother Cave Johnson. The brothers had travelled to the area earlier in the year hoping to take advantage of the ample land in the hitherto unsettled region. Upon arriving, the Johnsons joined a caravan of settlers and helped them to construct what would eventually become Bryan's Station. Having purchased around 5,000 acres of land from both Patrick Henry and James Madison, Robert Johnson settled along the Elkhorn River in the region of Kentucky, then still a part of the large colony of Virginia. His exploits in the Revolution continued and were only amplified after resettling and he is recorded as having taken part in George Rogers Clark's 1781–1782 campaign against the Miami and Shawnee Indians of Ohio.[3]

The year 1780 saw the unfolding of a massive British operation to re-take the entire western region of British America from the province of Quebec to New Orleans. One of the parts of this four pronged invasion was Captain Henry Bird's campaign against the area of Kentucky. Accompanied by around 500 Indians, Bird crossed the Ohio River and moved against Ruddle's Station on the Licking River. Though the local commander surrendered, Bird was unable to prevent the Natives under his command from tearing, "the poor children from their mothers' breasts, killed and wounded many."[4] Martin's Station next felt the wrath of the Indians before Bird called off the campaign for various reasons, choosing not to proceed against Lexington. Kentucky was thus temporarily saved from complete destruction. With the failure of the other three offensives as well, local commander George Rogers Clark decided to focus his efforts on pursuing and decimating Bird and his allies.

Clark led a massive raid across the Ohio River consisting of 1,000 men including Robert Johnson. The Kentuckians fought the only battle on Ohio soil during the Revolution when they encountered a group of Natives at Piqua in August 1780. After some minor fighting in which less than 50 men in total were killed, the Americans proceeded to burn some fields and buildings before returning across the river to Kentucky.

The origins of the name Kentucky have been the subject of heated debate for centuries, with little agreement. The first historian of the state, John Filson, writing in 1784 described the area as, "now called Kentucke, but known to the Indians by the name of the Dark and Bloody Ground, and sometimes as the Middle Ground ... Hence this fertile spot became an object of contention, a theater of war, from which it was properly denominated the Bloody Ground."[5] Even the Indians recognized early on the plentiful hunting to be had in the region. Numerous tribes fought each other and the Europeans upon their arrival for the rights to the area. Thus, far from removing his growing family from the dangers of war, Robert Johnson was instead placing them on the front lines of an even older conflict.

Robert Johnson proceeded in late 1779 with his family to Kentucky. Moving by water they wintered at Redstone, or Brownsville, before finally reaching Beargrass by the spring. Years later, Cave Johnson recorded the dangers that confronted the early colonists at this time.

> "And here I will mention another incident which occurred while he resided at Beargrass. The Indians had waylaid the trace that led from the settlement on Beargrass to the Falls, and had killed several people there. Having understood from the spies that were sent out to examine the neighborhood that they had discovered Indian signs, and that they apprehended they might be waylaying that trace, the inhabitants at the Falls and those of the Beargrass settlement raised a company and undertook to examine said trace. They divided into three companies. One marched along the trace, the other two marched through the woods on each side. They found the Indians, as they expected, lying in ambush near the road, and, coming on their backs, fired on them, killing one dead on the spot and wounding one other that got off. The Indians, discovering the men on the trace, fired at them at the same time they

were fired on, and wounded one of the white men badly. My brother Robert was one of the men who fired at the Indians."[6]

It was here amidst the constant threat of massacre by Native Americans that Richard Mentor Johnson was born on October 17, 1780. Stories of him being the first white child born in the territory are fanciful at best. In addition, despite later claiming that he was, "born in a cane-brake and cradled in a sap trough," Johnson's early years, though dangerous, were hardly that poverty stricken.[7] Having helped to survey huge tracts of the area since the 1780s, Robert Johnson was in fact one of the largest landowners in the state. By 1792, he and John Craig had bought up around 144,000 acres, and Johnson is recorded in the Census of 1810 as owning 32 slaves.[8] Settled along the Elkhorn Creek, the family, though economically prosperous, was still dependent upon the protection of the local fort in times of trouble. In this dangerous environment, Col. Johnson rightly took every opportunity to instill discipline and fortitude into his sons. According to one contemporary biography, the elder Johnson once had his sickly 15-year-old son James effectively carried into battle on a litter so that he could win his spurs in combat against the Natives.[9]

Various Indian groups under the command of the vilified frontier traitor Simon Girty ravaged the Kentucky area during the Revolution, including as part of Bird's failed offensive of 1780. Girty had been kidnapped as a youth by the Seneca and had been adopted into their tribe. Though initially dedicated to the American cause, by 1779 he had become a Loyalist, leading Native bands to attack frontier settlements for the British. The Johnson family, except for Robert who had been elected to the state legislature and was away in Richmond, was present at the fortified settlement of Bryan Station in modern day Lexington in August 1782 when English officer Capt. William Caldwell and Girty accompanied by hundreds of Indians and British soldiers attacked.[10] This collection of 40 log cabins was located about five miles from Lexington and would witness the opening salvo of the last major campaign of the American Revolution.[11]

Various apocryphal stories exist as to what transpired during this assault. One well-known tale has a flaming arrow being shot through the window of the Johnson household, burying itself into the side of the infant Richard's crib. Only the efforts of his 10-year-old sister Betsy allegedly saved the future Vice-President from death. Another story has Richard's older brother James being hoisted to the roof with a jug of water to put out the numerous reoccurring fires that afflicted the house, as he was, "too little to handle guns, but too big to be idle in such an emergency."[12] Most likely Mrs. Johnson and the other women of the settlement spent the time casting bullets for the men engaged in the desperate defense of the stockade. Yet the ever-present hot August sun and the periodic barrages of flaming arrows from the Indians, both soon made water a scarce resource.

The settlers usually relied upon a close by spring for their water needs, about 60 yards beyond the walls of the fort. Yet with the enemy concealed in the woods around the water source, its acquisition during the siege proved to be a problem. Reduced to dire straits, a proposal was made by Capt. John Craig to send the women and children out for water.[13] The apparent thought being that the Native Americans would not stoop to slaughtering unarmed women, or think that it was some sort of trap, or that the Indians would assume that the decision to send out women showed how confident the settlers were, thus spreading fear among the besiegers. Regardless of the motive, a dozen women and an equal number of children all led by Jemima Johnson boldly marched out of the stockade, filled their buckets, and returned to the settlement. The Indians, apparently confused by the jovial nature of the water party whose members talked and laughed as if oblivious to the siege, remained in hiding and did not launch an attack.

The Women of Bryant's Station Ky. supplying the Garrison with Water.

Image 1. The Women of Bryant's Station

Years later in 1896, the local chapter of the Daughters of the American Revolution constructed a monument on the site, though around the wrong spring, to commemorate this little known but unique action during the war for independence.[14] It is not surprising therefore that one writer once referred to Jemima Johnson as, "the bravest woman in all frontier history."[15] Memories and stories of her actions, undoubtedly repeated time and time again around the family hearth, certainly inspired the future Vice-President.

With colonial reinforcements slowly arriving and the walls of the fort proving to be too stout for his limited artillery, Caldwell eventually decided to abandon the siege. Instead he and Girty opted to draw the Kentuckians into an ambush at the nearby Blue Licks. The colonials brazenly followed, accompanied by the famous tracker Daniel Boone, and in the end almost half of the force was killed or captured. This disastrous loss served to depopulate Bryan Station, and when combined

7

with the opportunities offered by the ending of the war, pushed to disperse the settlers to surrounding lands. The Johnson family was one of these groups and soon moved to establish a permanent residence elsewhere in the territory.

In retaliation for the British and Indian assault on Kentucky, George Rogers Clark led a campaign deep into Ohio and Illinois in the fall of 1782. Robert Johnson was present at these battles as well, helping to defeat the Miami and Shawnee. In November of that year alone, he participated in the burning of a number of Indian villages including those at Piqua, Chillicothe, Willstown, McKee's Town, and Standing Stone.[16] Yet Detroit remained out of reach for the Americans and most of the Indians simply withdrew. With the Revolution coming to a close, this proved to be the last major campaign in not only the western theater, but the war as well.

The Johnson family grew more influential in the Kentucky region after the war. Johnson's Fort was constructed in 1783 after the family had left Bryan Station and moved a dozen miles to the north, settling near the Elkhorn. This stockade would eventually develop into the town of Great Crossing next to modern day Georgetown, named for an old bison trail that led to the Ohio River. Robert Johnson rose in rank and status due to his martial accomplishments largely against the Natives of the "Bloody Ground." Expeditions continued to be launched in retaliation for Indian raids throughout the 1780s. In late 1786, Robert took the opportunity to write James Madison that, "we have at present an Expedition Gone against the wabach Indins to the amt. of abt. 1200 Men and another to march in two Days against the Shawnees, who have Broke the articles of the treaty by stealing and Killing proved by Substantial witnesses."[17] Yet despite any success, Kentucky was back at war only three years later.

> "About the 10th instant two men were fired on by a party of Indians but no damage sustained only one of the horses the men rode was killed: the Indians took the saddle & bridle and the night following they stole eleven horses, our men pursued them next day came up with them and retook all the horses, together with

said saddle & bridle, and killed two (one of which was a white man). On Sunday the 16th six negroes were taken by a party of Indians in ambuscade about three quarters of a mile from my house. they carried them about one quarter of a mile where they were suprised by the noise of some people riding near them, they tomahawked four, two of which died, two was left for dead which is now in a hopeful way of recovery; the other two made their escape while they were murdering the rest."[18]

Johnson went on to inform both the President and Vice President of retaliatory raids launched by the residents of the region.

"The day following the party was seen twice and the evening or night of the sixteenth they stole some horses from captain Buford we pursued them as quick as possible with about forty men to the Ohio, about twenty five miles below the mouth of Big Miami, where twenty six volunteers crossed the Ohio after them, we came to a large camp of them early in the morning of the 20th about twelve miles from the Ohio, we divided our party and attacked them opposite, on each side, they fought us a short time in that position until they got their women & children out of the way, and then give back to a thick place of high weeds & bushes, where they hid very close we immediately drove up about forty of their horses and made our retreat across the Ohio, we lost three men & two wounded. The Indians wounded one of our men as we returned. Thus they are going on from time to time in this country."[19]

Seeking help from the national government, Johnson took the opportunity to write to a variety of important persons. To Governor Beverley Randolph of Virginia he related how, "the hostile acts of the Indians is so frequent that it becomes troublesome to write to you on every occasion."[20] In fact by 1789, over a thousand Americans had been killed along the frontier by marauding bands of Native Americans. His entreaties, among others, seem to have had the desired effect for in April of 1790 Secretary of War Henry Knox wrote to Johnson informing him that President Washington thanks him for the information and has approved the raising of local troops to battle the Indians.[21]

The resulting war became known as the Northwest Indian War and saw the young republic engaged for a decade against a loose coalition of Indian tribes. In 1790, General Josiah Harmar wrote in a letter that he was preparing an offensive largely off of the warnings and input of Robert Johnson.[22] The general then built an army of around 1,500 men, two-thirds of whom were militia from Kentucky and Pennsylvania. Unfortunately though, poor leadership and the rawness of the recruits led to hundreds of American deaths in one of the worst defeats in American history. The war would continue until 1795 after which Robert Johnson would come under attack from the Department of War for various financial irregularities pertaining to his raising and equipping of units.[23] This would not be the last time that the Johnson family was accused of misusing tax payer money.

Robert Johnson's growing prestige predictably led to his election to the Virginia state legislature in 1782 representing Fayette County, one of the three original counties of Kentucky. Yet the local democracy movement that had arisen as part of the Revolution slowly began to work against the sheer size of the state of Virginia. For a variety of reasons, one of which was the inability of the Virginia government to respond effectively to the Indian incursions into the western lands, the people of Kentucky began to push for the creation of their own state during the waning days of the Revolution.[24] The two regions had become economically, socially, and even politically separate entities, with the residents of Kentucky being largely small farmers who were almost entirely opposed to the adoption of the Constitution while the eastern regions of Virginia were more inclined to it. It was no surprise that Col. Johnson was then selected to represent the people of the region during a statehood convention in 1785. He informed Madison of the prospect by letter, stating that, "our convention is To sit in a few Days and it is Expected we Shall Diturmine upon a Separation and of course Have another Eli[c]tion to Diturmine on what Laws Shall Gover[n] us after the separation and to Do the Great business of forming a Constitution." He went on to beseech Madison that, "I hope You wil be a frien[d] to our petition and if you would take the trouble by letter to Give me or some others in this Country your advice in forming a constitution with Some observations and objections which You probably May have against the Virginia Constitution."[25]

Yet it would take many years, numerous failed conventions, and even the threat of secession by rebellion before Virginia finally relented and granted the area its independence in 1792. Once again we see Robert Johnson serving as a member of the constitutional convention, helping to draft the founding document of the new state. At various points a state senator or representative, he became an ardent Jeffersonian Republican and opposed such measures as the re-chartering of the Bank of the United States and the expansion of the federal government. The elder Johnson remained involved in both local and national politics for years, carrying on a steady correspondence with many notable political figures.[26]

Robert remained in the state legislature for a number of years while at the same time becoming a wealthy planter in the region. In 1805, he undertook to establish a landing on the Ohio River to serve as an outlet for the produce and products of Scott County. Nine years later, he purchased enough land to turn this port into a town named Fredericksburg, subsequently renamed Warsaw in 1831, downriver from Covington and Cincinnati.

All throughout this time Robert Johnson sought to push the political and social advancement of his children. His two daughters each married successful generals, with Elizabeth being wedded to John Payne who was present at the Battle of Yorktown and would serve at the Battle of the Thames with Richard and his brother, and Sarah marrying Gen. William T. Ward (1769–1839). The Wards would go on to become some of the largest landowners in the Mississippi Delta region after the removal of most of the Choctaw Indians, with William Ward himself serving as the Indian Agent for the tribe from 1821–1833.

Robert's sons worked towards equaling him in both political and economic success. Some became acclaimed military officers and heroes, others rose through the political ranks in all three branches of local or federal government, and still others built up mercantile empires. Opponents of the family at the time quipped that the Johnsons looked for, "power in every hole and corner of the state." They were in many ways the first democratic political dynasty in the nation, the Kennedys of the antebellum period, far surpassing their contemporaries the Adams in numbers and power. Numerous nephews and nieces and cousins would go on to play important roles in politics, the military, business, and even fight on both sides in the Civil War. Yet no one in the family would look harder for power, or find it more readily, than did Richard Mentor Johnson.

If Richard Johnson's birth was amidst the violence that witnessed the creation of the country, then his growth paralleled that of the nation as well. The ending of the war for independence saw relative peace return to Kentucky and with it a certain level of prosperity. Though periodic Indian attacks would continue, these were largely quieted down following the Northwest Indian War of the 1790s. The Johnsons became rather respectable members of frontier society, with young Richard learning the life and skills of a yeoman farmer. His first 16 years were largely spent laboring on the family property helping to provide for his brothers and sisters. A political biography published in the 1840s delved into great detail regarding his assorted horticultural, frontier, and industrial skills; areas in which he excelled well beyond those around him. "He excelled in industry. No youth of his age could rival him in cutting down trees, mauling rails, ploughing the ground, hoeing the corn, or reaping the harvest field."[27] Clearly, this campaign literature was simply aimed at portraying him to be a potential "log cabin president" in the best image of Andrew Jackson. In reality, life on a well-staffed plantation would have taught him few physical skills, but may have instilled in him lessons in leadership and the management of men. These proficiencies would in the end prove to be far more valuable to his future than the splitting of wood.

At the age of 16, young Richard left the family farm to attend a local grammar school. After acquiring a rudimentary education in English and Latin, Johnson was admitted to Transylvania University. A Kentucky historian once described the early days of the school as being, "often disturbed by the yell of the Indian and the crack of his rifle ...

the roll of the drum called many a youth from the quiet of the school-house, and the turbulence of the times often forced him to exchange books for rifle and tomahawk."[28] The Virginia Legislature had established the school, the first college west of the Allegheny Mountains, in 1780. Thus, despite its peripheral status, Transylvania University was in fact one of the oldest colleges in the nation. The school itself could boast of not only Richard Johnson as an alumni, but dozens of other politicians as well. Included among these were Jefferson Davis, Stephen Austin, John C. Breckinridge, Albert Sidney Johnston, 50 senators, and 36 governors. Nor was he the only member of the Johnson family to attend the school as at least one brother, John Telemachus, and numerous nephews were matriculated there as well. Richard's father had been a trustee of the school in 1783, no doubt helping to ease his son's entrance a decade later. This was not the only institution sponsored by Robert Johnson. During his lifetime he also helped to establish the Rittenhouse Academy and the Kentucky Society for promoting useful information. The family's strong belief in education was a trait carried on through the actions of both Richard Mentor and John Telemachus in later years. Finally, most of these institutions had a religious bent to them, in this case Baptist, though the partnership of religion and education was very common at the time.

While at the school, Johnson studied law under Col. George Nicholas, the father of Kentucky's constitution and the state's first attorney general. Following the death of that great man in 1799, Richard next learned from James Brown, the former secretary of state for Kentucky and a future United States Senator for the state of Louisiana. Both men had themselves studied under the legendary George Wythe who had also taught law to Jefferson, Marshall, and Clay. Though his official campaign biography lamented the, "disadvantages of a hurried education," and Benjamin Perley Poore once described him as, "slightly educated," he seems to have spent no more or no less time at the school than anyone else and managed to gain admittance to the bar in 1802.[29] His educational level appears to have been modest for while many of his best speeches and orations contained some classical and biblical references many were alleged to have been ghost written. He himself stressed that, "public speaking is not my forte," a sentiment agreed upon by some of his contemporaries.[30]

Patriotic zeal early on inhabited the heart of Johnson as he worked to organize a company of volunteers under his command in 1802 during the Spanish war scare while he was still at college.[31] That year the Spanish intendant at New Orleans closed the port to American shipping, a direct violation of Pinckney's Treaty. His father wrote to a number of people expressing Kentucky's dissatisfaction with Spanish actions.[32] Though the matter was resolved peacefully, the incident served as a dress rehearsal for later events involving Johnson. Perhaps Robert Johnson in a letter to Richard Livingston best expressed the thoughts of Kentuckians at the time ...

> "The assurances of Mr. Yrujo with other evidence, make it pretty certain that the measure of the Intendant was not warranted by orders from his Government, and it is hoped that the interpositions for correcting it will succeed before much injury will have ensued. The excitement however which it has produced ought to admonish the Holders whoever they may be, of the Mouth of the Mississippi, that justice, ample justice to the Western Citizens of the U. States, is the only tenure of peace with this Country. There are now or in two years will be, not less than 200,000 Militia on the waters of the Mississpi., every man of whom would march at a Minutes warning to remove obstructions from that outlet to the Sea, every man of whom regards the free use of that river as a natural & indefeasable right, and is conscious of the physical force that can at any time give effect to it."[33]

Upon returning triumphantly to his home from his studies, Richard was given a plantation and a collection of slaves by his father. Between his home at Blue Springs Farm, his country store at Great Crossings, and his growing legal business, Johnson quickly became a cornerstone in Kentucky society. His supporters and panegyrists claimed that he fought tirelessly on behalf of widows and orphans often, "without reward" during these early years.[34] While the selflessness of his legal career may be called into question, the youth of the state and its conflicting land grants assuredly led to numerous law suits that certainly occupied his time and talents. Regardless, Johnson's lineage, education, wealth, and attributes promised that he would not long remain on his farm or in small-town life.

Robert's wife Jemima would die on March 23, 1814, followed by her husband a little over a year later on October 15, 1815. Both would subsequently be buried at Great Crossing in Scott County in what became the Johnson family cemetery. It was now up to Richard and the first born generation of Kentuckians to continue the march towards progress, a march that would ultimately lead them to the city of Washington.

CHAPTER II

MR. JOHNSON GOES TO WASHINGTON

"But still prouder is he to be called an American Republican; for there is nothing sectional in his feelings. He regards the different States as members of one body, no one of which can suffer injury without inflicting pain on the whole, nor one enjoy prosperity without benefiting the whole."[35] Despite this lofty praise from a contemporary, partisan biographer, Johnson was no more of a staunch nationalist or less of a regional proponent than most other politicians of the time period. He grew to maturity as a typical frontier Jeffersonian much like his father, eager to expand the nation in order to open up new lands and opportunities to settlers while at the same time a jealous defender of the rights of his state. His belief in limited government is best exemplified by a speech he gave during the debate on the Missouri Compromise.

> "Competent or not, the people of Missouri have the right, and they must exercise it without any restriction which is not common to all the States. If you begin to prescribe restrictions, you may pursue the course without limitation or control. You may prescribe the qualifications of electors and candidates the powers and organization of every branch of their government, till self-government is lost, and their liberty is but an empty name."[36]

This unique western philosophy would serve him well as a moderator between northern and southern interests in the coming years. At best, Richard Mentor Johnson was a democratic politician in the truest sense of the phrase, representing the collective will of the majority of the people at the time, paying only occasional heed to the philosophical underpinning of their demands. A Whig on some issues, a Democrat on others, but always a Kentuckian.

Johnson's first attempt at gaining political office failed when in 1803 he was defeated by two other Republicans, Gen. Thomas Sandford and William Henry, for a Congressional seat. Though it was not unheard of in the western states at that time for a man of his youth and relative inexperience to be elected to national office, his lack of qualifications proved to be too much of a hindrance on this occasion. Sandford as a veteran of the Revolution was certainly thought to be a safer and more accomplished choice for office. Yet experience was not the only attribute sought after by the electorate as at the same time his father was twice turned away from a position as Lt. Governor of the state in 1800 and 1804. The renown of his family, when combined with his own merits, finally secured his election to the state legislature at the age of 23, a more appropriate office for someone of his limited accomplishments than the House of Representatives.

Johnson's ascent to power at this time was aided by a similar movement among young Republicans across the nation, buttressed in part by the recent accomplishments of President Jefferson. The Revolution of 1800 not only brought Jefferson into office but carried Johnson and other young, like minded men of democratic values in its wake as well. Though technically the Kentucky state constitution mandated an age of 24 to serve in the legislature, Johnson was seated with little protest. "The desire of his fellow-citizens that he should serve them, caused a suppression of all inquiry as to the qualification of age."[37] The ambiguities of records in the region most likely also played into his successful seating as the first native born Kentuckian in that body. In fact a similar occurrence happened around the same time to Henry Clay who though not yet 30 years of age had been selected to serve in the Kentucky Senate.

The young Johnson's time in the Kentucky legislature was a good introduction to many of the same issues that he would encounter during his later career. Local banking, land sales, debt repayment, and voting rights were all topics of the day. One of his earliest recorded votes of importance came in late November 1805 when he supported a proposal by Henry Clay to strip voting rights from legislators who owed money to the state for land purchases. This piece of legislation arose from an effort by Clay and others to stop the dissolution of the Kentucky Insurance Company by the state. Efforts were underway by the

Senate of Kentucky to strip away its banking privileges, a move reflective of the larger anti-U.S. Bank atmosphere within the nation. Clay's bill successfully convinced enough legislators to withdraw their opposition to the company as many of them were deeply in debt from land purchases. It is impossible to say if Johnson's support for the measure arose from his hatred of a central bank, a desire to strip votes away from Federalist legislators, or simply an early attachment to Clay's rising star.

The Johnson family as a whole became intimately acquainted early on with Henry Clay. Robert Johnson was a party to several lawsuits also involving Clay over the numerous confused land deals that plagued the early years of the state. Clay was even hired by Robert to serve as an arbitrator in several of these suits. In addition, James Johnson wrote to Clay on January 28, 1809, congratulating his fellow Kentuckian for his, "firmness and courage," in his recent, famous duel with Humphrey Marshall. "This will serve to stop the mouths of all snivel faced Tories."[38] Years later during a campaign stop in Harrisburg in 1840, Vice President Richard Johnson recalled how, "the first time he ever remembered taking off his coat to fight was with Henry Clay against the supporters of the alien and sedition laws. He said that in argument Mr. Clay wielded a battle axe, while he could only handle a tomahawk."[39]

Though some in the west at that time favored secession or disunion for the region in order to allow it to pursue its own path, Johnson was a staunch unionist. He delivered an address back in January 1807 while still a member of the Kentucky legislature condemning Aaron Burr's attempts to seize the recently acquired Louisiana Purchase. His own father had written to Madison in 1802 expressing his distrust of Burr, "I have strong suspisions of Mr. Burr, from severall circumstances, & think it will be unsafe to run him with Mr. Jefeson for the next Presidenty."[40] The Johnsons were firm supporters of the rights of individuals, but always within the framework of the nation-state. This mindset would follow the younger Johnson throughout his days in Washington and be reflected in his numerous writings and speeches on the issues of slavery, the Missouri and California compromise, and the impending breakup of the states.

Yet Richard's initial defeats for national office did not dampen his efforts to get elected to Congress, after all the state legislature was no place for a man with his level of personal drive and ambition. In 1806, Johnson won election to the House of Representatives for Kentucky's 4th Congressional District after serving little more than two years at the state level. In a three-way race Johnson defeated his past rival Thomas Sandford, the then sitting Congressman, and James Moore to represent Shelby, Scott, and Franklin counties. Once again in a repeat of history, Richard Mentor Johnson was constitutionally too young on the day of the election in August to hold his appointed seat. Yet unlike in 1804, the matter proved to be less of an issue as by the time Johnson took his seat in March 1807, he had attained the proper age. In fact the Congress that he was first seated in, the 10th, was unique in American history. Seventy new members were elected that year, almost half of the total body, many of whom were under the age of 40. This new, young Congress complimented well the hopes and vitality of an equally fresh, vibrant nation.[41]

The young Kentuckian would go on to serve in the House from 1807 to 1819, exposing himself early on as an advocate of Jeffersonian Republicanism. His efforts towards reducing the suffering of debtors and of eliminating the power of organized religion over the state were all elements of classical Jeffersonian thought. He was after all a student of the Age of Enlightenment, recording years later how he made a pilgrimage to visit Thomas Paine only a few weeks before that famous writer's death in 1809.[42] Much later during a birthday celebration for Paine thrown by Tammany Hall, Johnson's name was prominent in both speeches and impromptu toasts in association with that of the Revolutionary.[43]

Yet Johnson's defense of Jefferson and his philosophy almost cost him his life in 1811. Kentucky Federalist John McKinley had compared President Jefferson to George III and Napoleon during a dinner. Richard's brother James, who had himself been elected to the Kentucky Senate, shortly afterward published a letter savagely attacking McKinley which led the latter to apparently engage him in a street brawl in October in Georgetown, Kentucky. Though the older Johnson came out the victor, Richard published a series of handbills ridiculing and insulting McKinley for his conduct. Yet after being challenged by both

McKinley as well as his fellow Federalist Humphrey Marshall to duels, Richard declined both on flimsy excuses and quickly returned to Washington.[44] As previously mentioned, Clay himself had also dueled with Marshall in 1809 over the latter's Anglophile views and had even received a congratulatory letter from James Johnson.

Historically, Johnson was a member of the clique known as the War Hawks, a group of young, southern and western Republicans dedicated to the expansion and development of the nation rather than its division or dissolution. Fellow Kentuckian Henry Clay, Peter Buell Porter of New York, and South Carolinians John C. Calhoun and Langdon Cheves were also prominent members of Congress who held to the same ideas and the various men, at least early on, worked towards common goals. Yet during Jefferson's presidency this group was a clear minority within the House. In fact it was only the ardent belief in nationalism, individual determination, and persuasive legislative practices of these War Hawks that allowed them to push forward their platform. By December 1811, they even managed to win the Speakership for one of their number, Johnson's fellow Kentuckian Henry Clay. The War Hawks would retain control over the leadership of the House from 1811 to 1820 as the Speakership alternated between Clay and Cheves. Britain became the natural target of these early believers in Manifest Destiny as it consistently violated the rights and territorial integrity of the new nation. In fact Johnson's first appearance in Congress came following a call for it to assemble by then Pres. Jefferson in response to the Chesapeake-Leopard Affair. This infamous event would serve as one of the major impetuses for the War of 1812.

Early on during his time in the House, Johnson busied himself as chairman of the Committee on Pension and Revolutionary War Claims. This body had formed in 1813 to replace the Committee on Claims and as such its bailiwick included all pension and damage claims relating to the Revolution. Undoubtedly Johnson, as a self-proclaimed champion of the common man, thought this an ideal position for his talents. In addition, the patronage and positive press that he would acquire from doling out funds would certainly help to further his career. He quite early on achieved a certain level of notoriety, in fact, for his attempts to properly distribute land and money to all those affected by the war, even when their politics clashed with his own. Most notable among the many claims that he pushed was that of Alexander Hamilton's widow. Regardless of Hamilton's controversial status to Republicans as the head of the Federalist Party, Johnson pushed for the rights of his wife to collect money due to him. Unfortunately in the end though, the Republican dominated Committee refused her pleas. As a newspaper eulogized him shortly after his death, "he was not controlled by party or personal ties in such matters. He served and aided the suffering of all parties and circles."[45] While the Chairman's actions may have been heroically retold by later supporters as examples of his bipartisan nature, they most likely were couched by the fact that he knew the committee would never approve Elizabeth Schuyler Hamilton's claims, thus allowing him to gallantly defend her in committee. Ultimately though, according to various campaign biographers, Johnson became frustrated by the limitations of the committee and eventually resigned. More likely he realized the limited progress that could be made chairing such a minor committee and sought a more desirable position.

Johnson continued to win re-election to the House, serving from 1807 to 1819. Sometimes he ran unopposed and sometimes he competed with other Republicans, but in no case was his return to Congress ever in doubt. Politics in the state of Kentucky mirrored those of the larger nation at this time. The Republican Party dominated the state's representation in both houses of Congress from the election of Jefferson until the Election of 1824. Yet despite being merely another western Republican in a sea of many, he early on came to the notice of the administration. The influential Baptist preacher, Rev. George Eve touted him in a letter to James Madison in 1807, "he is a worthy young man and from the acquaintance existing between us I shall esteem it as fredly if you will be of that advantage to him that is in your power."[46]

As was previously mentioned, Johnson's arrival in the House coincided with one of the darkest moments in Anglo-American relations. On June 22, 1807, the British warship *HMS Leopard* opened fire upon the smaller American frigate *USS Chesapeake* after the latter refused her demands to turn over suspected deserters. Following a fierce cannonade and the death of four Americans, Capt. Barron of the Chesapeake was forced to yield and allow his ship to be boarded by the British. The event quickly aroused a feeling of anti-British sentiment and hatred unfelt since the fight over Jay's Treaty a decade before. Calls for revenge or war were heard from many corners of the republic. Even a letter in a Federalist newspaper out of Frankfort, *The Western World,* expressed the feeling that America would not be safe and secure, "until the flag with thirteen stripes shall adorn the ramparts of Quebec."[47]

In response, President Jefferson decided to retaliate in an economic rather than physical fashion. This decision ultimately produced the Embargo Act of 1807, a document that would only further push America towards war. Ever the loyal party man, Johnson voted for the controversial piece of legislation, confident not only in its effectiveness but also apparently unconcerned with the economic devastation that would follow. He was possibly also influenced by the fact that as the legislation would have a positive effect on domestic manufacturing it was seen by many as favoring western states such as Kentucky.

The act produced financial depression and outrage in New England and threatened to devastate the Republican Party in the next elections. As attacks on both the act and Jefferson started to increase in newspapers and on the floor of Congress, Johnson and others soon found themselves called on to defend their vote. Following a particularly vehement verbal assault by Barent Gardenier of New York, Johnson leapt to his feet to accuse the Congressman of slander.[48] Calls to rescind the legislation for both economic and political reasons began to grow louder. In response, many Congressmen changed sides and abandoned the President's policy. Johnson himself, unsure of which way to turn, called upon Jefferson personally for advice. Allegedly Jefferson wrote the following to Johnson in reply ...

> "Mr. Johnson, when I was of your age, I thought like you in matters of policy; that is, that measures calculate to promote the welfare of the country should be persisted in while a majority would sustain them, however great might be the minority, or however violent their opposition; but the experience of years has convinced me that it is not always wise to do so. In a democratic republic, where the mass of the people of

all parties have the same interest at stake, some respect must be had to the feelings and wishes of the minority, especially when the minority is large and clamorous; otherwise, it will be impossible to avoid discord, and discord weakens the bonds of union. This embargo, I doubt not, if still persisted in, would save our country from war, and secure our right upon the ocean; but the opposition is so great and violent, and still increasing, that it threatens a worse state of things at home than would result from a foreign rupture."[49]

Jefferson's concern for the rights of the minority, though quite uncharacteristic of the party's often stated philosophical position on the will of the majority, was perhaps more a result of the same pragmatism that led him to continue the Bank of the United States and led him to purchase Louisiana, ideas quite opposed to his philosophies upon taking office. For his own part, Johnson would often write to Jefferson over the next few years to seek advice from the sage of Monticello. Johnson's fawning over Jefferson is clearly evident in a letter from February 27, 1808, which though ostensibly written as a basic letter of recommendation for a position in Louisiana Territory, quickly turns into a paean on the President.

"Permit me to say, that I have been taught from my Infancy to revere your Character, and respect your political Course which has contributed so much to the permanent freedom of the U States & of which americans are proud to boast—The more I know of your long & faithful services, & the Measures of your administration, the greater is my attachment to them & you. I am convinced, that your enemies consist principally of Tories, British Hirelings, Aristocrats, Monarchists, & the political Apostates—Tho' you are shielded from their abuse, I confess I read & hear it with indignation—I have no excuse to make for such malignant and unworthy beings—They are our political enemies—I shall ever regret the moment you leave the Councils of the U. States. I feel in you a confidence, & an attachment which is indescribable, & can never be excelled—Your administration has given stability to those principles, which can alone settle upon a firm basis the American Republic—& will remain as a monument of your services—You are and ever will live in the affections of your Country. These impressions can only testify my own feelings—& can add nothing to your happiness. I hope they will be received, as evidence of a youthful attachment, which I hope will increase with my years."[50]

Fifteen months later when Congress replaced the Embargo Act at Jefferson's suggestion with the Non-intercourse Act of 1809, Johnson and the other War Hawks whole heartedly supported that legislation as well. Yet this proved to be no more effective or enforceable than the previous piece of legislation and did little to stop the slow slide to war of the United States.

During this time Richard Mentor Johnson remained a staunch opponent of the Bank of the United States as well. A perennial target for Republicans since the birth of the two party system, the bank as established by Alexander Hamilton was seen to epitomize the anti-egalitarianism of the Federalist Party. Southerners and westerners despised the corruption inherent in the system and resented the bank's focus on the Northeast. After 20 years in existence, the Bank of the United States' charter came up for renewal in March 1811. Representative Johnson took this opportunity to express his hatred of the institution.

He argued that the bank should not be renewed as it was unconstitutional, improper, and inexpedient.

"This is not a struggle, on our part, to repeal any act of incorporation, or to deprive any citizen of any vested rights claimed either by nature or by any political act; but an exertion in favor of equal laws and equal justice to all the people of the United States, to prevent monopolies from being given to a moneyed aristocracy, unknown to the constitution, and dangerous to the liberties of the people, and subversive of the State sovereignties."[51]

In his speech on the subject before the House, Johnson advances himself as a follower and defender of the Constitution in the strict constructionist sense of Jefferson, arguing that the government should restrict itself to only those duties so outlined by that document. "The people are republican, and they abhor all measures of a monarchical tendency."[52] To many Republicans, the Bank represented a dangerous consolidation of power by the federal government.

> "Sir, it will be difficult to convince the people that it is necessary, in the language of the Constitution, to create a moneyed aristocracy and a privileged order of men, extending its branches, its influence, and its strength, into the interior of every State, to collect taxes, to borrow money, or to regulate commerce. The primary object of this incorporation was to promote usurpation of power, to support the dangerous doctrine of implication, and to amass wealth from the labor of the people, and not for the exclusive object of carrying into effect any express authority in the Constitution."[53]

Not only did Johnson doubt the Bank's constitutionality, he feared its reach of power due to the very methods used to ensure its re-chartering. "To induce us to vote for this institution, we have been persuaded, flattered, alarmed, petitioned, and threatened, and we have been amused with the rise and history of the banking system."[54] Nor could he resist once again revisiting the debate over the Embargo Act, blaming price fluctuations in the West not on fears of the Bank's dissolution but on the peoples' dependence on foreign commerce.

After countering what he sees as the oft provided defenses for the chartering of the Bank, Johnson finished his address with a dire warning against the future of the country should it be in the hands of moneyed corporations.

> "If we die with less money, we shall live in more honor and enjoy more happiness. I wish to see whether so much depends upon this corporation ... Like the strong man we read of in Holy Writ, let us see if the violent death of this corporate body will pull down the

pillars of the Constitution, that another Volney may sit upon the ruins of this capital, and mourn the fallen empire of this great and happy republic."[55]

Johnson's belief in the man rather than the institution would be borne out with his actions during the War of 1812.

CHAPTER III
THE WAR THAT MADE THE MAN

As one historian has pointed out, "there was then in Kentucky—and would continue to be—a class of men whose fetish was bravado. Mostly of families imbued with the old traditions of the Virginia Tidewater, they had brought their carefully sustained reputations for daring into the wilderness."[56] The Johnsons were certainly one of those families, both in lineage and in action. In fact the defining moment in Richard Mentor Johnson's life, and that of many of his brothers, was certainly their involvement in the War of 1812. What Republicans at the time termed America's Second Revolution was not only a rebirth for the nation, but for many up to that point unknown Americans as well. While historians and politicians may debate the outcome of the conflict and argue over the gains made by either side, it is certain that Johnson emerged from the war a changed man and a national hero. Tales of his battles, his leadership qualities, and his personal defeat of Tecumseh would be the catalyst for all that was to follow.

Confrontation between the United Kingdom and the United States had been building for the better part of a decade. As previously discussed, the former nation's policy of impressment had brought the two counties close to war numerous times during the presidency of Thomas Jefferson. Johnson closely followed the events with England, including the mission of George H. Rose whom the British sent as a special minister in 1808 to resolve the issues arising from the Chesapeake Leopard Affair. Yet Rose's mission ultimately ended in failure as he was unwilling and unable to discuss the issue of impressment. In a letter written to his fellow Kentuckian Adam Beatty, Johnson noted that, "when you read his note to Mr. Madison you would suppose that he crossed the ocean to complain & demand concession from us rather than to make any atonement."[57] To the young Kentuckian the issue was clearly one of America as the injured party. He once unflatteringly referred in Congress to Canada as nothing more than a, "rogues' harbor."[58] Nor was Johnson to be bullied into silence by his more senior colleagues.

During the debate on the issue of British aggression John Randolph, Congressman from Virginia and leader of the Tertium Quids, challenged Johnson that if he, "prove his assertions, I will join him in an expedition to Canada to avenge the wrong."[59] The young Congressman from Kentucky thereafter frequently reminded Randolph of his promise after war was declared, much to the humor of his colleagues.

As the Embargo Act and Non-intercourse Act both failed to defuse the situation, anger and frustration on the part of many citizens turned to thoughts of war. Yet not all of the War Hawks were intent on war at all costs. Johnson himself in a letter to then Secretary of State James Madison wrote that, "The people are willing to Suffer every privation which pacific measures may produce, or actively take up arms in Defence of their nation. The confidence of the people in the administration increases."[60] The Congressman from Kentucky was always careful to balance his interests in expansion and his desire to stand up for the rights of the nation with the knowledge of the destruction that war would bring to the frontier. His opposition to Campbell's Report, which was delivered in front of the House on November 22, 1808, and which blatantly recommended war, serves to prove this.[61] Undoubtedly his and his family's experiences with frontier war in early Kentucky helped to shape this mindset.

For western War Hawks, there was a more compelling reason than impressment to seek war with England. The Native threat to the region did not begin or end with the Northwestern Indian War of the 1790s. Rather the conflict had actually entered a new stage at this time as the porous and undefined border between Canada and the United States became used by a new Indian confederation in order to raid American settlements and then withdraw to where they could not be pursued.

The most recent confrontation between the two arose in 1810 out of opposition to the Treaty of Ft. Wayne from Tecumseh and his brother the Prophet. After failing to convince William Henry Harrison, the territorial governor, to rescind the treaty, Tecumseh and his brother began to build an alliance of sympathetic tribes and procured shipments of weapons from over the Canadian border. Harrison marched north with a small army, including men from Kentucky, and in 1811 utterly defeated the Prophet at the famed Battle of Tippecanoe. Yet Tecumseh was still active, weapons continued to flow across the border, and the British were seen by many to be inciting the violence in the region. Though modern day residents of the Blue Grass State may not consider themselves to be close to Canada today, in 1812 it was effectively a border state touching upon the Indian inhabited wilds of the old northwest.

Pres. Madison ultimately presented a request for a declaration of war to Congress on June 1, 1812. After days of deliberation, the House passed a resolution by a vote of 79:49 while the Senate assented with an even closer 19:13. Not a single Federalist voted in favor of the conflict, nor did many Republicans in northern states. Representative Johnson, as a War Hawk, duly and unsurprisingly gave his approval to the war. A year later while engaged in a campaign against Canada he stated his reasons for doing so as not being out of anger towards the English, but towards their actions. "The inhabitants of Canada—we fight not to conquer them, but the policy which made them our enemies. May they soon be united to the American Republic."[62] The final phrase again shows his overall thinking to be couched in his belief in the philosophy of Manifest Destiny. In this Johnson was voting the will of his constituents as most Kentuckians favored the conflict. Behind this support were economic and political motives, but also social ones as well. The Baptist faith which was becoming more and more strongly entrenched in the region and within the Johnson family, favored war with England and saw opposition as stemming from Federalist Presbyterian resistance and collusion.[63]

The Election of 1812 later that year served as a referendum on the war with England. James Madison was heartily re-nominated by a Republican caucus that included as its party secretary, Richard Johnson. The President based his re-election around the issue of war while a fusion Federalist/Anti-war Republican ticket ran DeWitt Clinton of New York against him. Though the election proved to be the closest since 1800, the War Hawks and Madison carried the majority of the nation from Pennsylvania to the south. Though Federalists did pick up a few seats in the Senate, the Republicans maintained an almost two-third majority in both houses. Kentucky, like many other states, returned only Republicans to Congress in 1813. Richard Mentor Johnson himself ran unopposed and was returned to the House of Representatives as a prominent member of the War Hawk bloc.

During the summer between the declaration of war and his re-election to Congress in November, Johnson became extensively involved in the conflict. Only a week after war was declared, Johnson stood before Congress to recommend the raising of several hundred rangers in the west. "Mr. J. said he would not detain the House with that detailed information which he had received as to the extent of the calamity which had fallen upon the people of the frontier settlements and which would be more disastrous, if not arrested by greater force."[64] Once his motion had passed, and rather than sitting idly by, he proceeded to personally raise 300 volunteers in Kentucky, undoubtedly hoping for a federal commission in the much anticipated invasion of Canada. As he wrote to Madison in July, Kentuckians, "are a spirited people and nothing can satisfy them but some military enterprise ... when will our President permit our volunteers to Serve in the glorious cause of their Country."[65] His father Robert expressed a similar sentiment in a letter to Pres. Madison in September 1812, "some of the people of Kentucky expected when war [sic] was declared that 10,000 men would have been ordered to upper Canada to take that province and enex [sic] it to the United States, and at the Same time double the number or more ordered to lower Canada to prevent reinforcements from one place to the other."[66] The younger Johnson's actions were far from unique as this was truly a time period of Congressional valor when the public expected its elected officials to take the field in defense of them as readily as they did the rostra at the Capitol. His men duly elected him as the major of the battalion, and following its union with another similarly sized force he was named colonel. The unit was consolidated with others into a brigade under the command of General Edward W. Tupper of Ohio and soon after proceeded northwards.

One of the earliest engagements of the war, and the one which bore the most interest for the citizens of Kentucky, was the campaign taking place around Detroit. Having only recently recovered from a devastating fire that destroyed practically every building in the town, the capital of Michigan Territory boasted a population of around 1,600.

Since its settlement in 1701 Detroit served as an important point on the Canadian fur trade route and by the time of the Revolution was the third largest city in Quebec. Once war was declared Pres. Madison and Sec. of War Eustis urged Gen. William Hull, the most senior officer in the area, to both strengthen the defenses of Detroit and to launch an invasion of western Ontario. The latter move, it was believed, would also hopefully relieve pressure on the main offensives being undertaken over the New York border.

Though Hull undoubtedly had serious misgivings about such a movement due to the shape and state of his forces, he nonetheless crossed the Detroit River on July 12. After some minor skirmishing and the issuance of various proclamations, Gen. Hull proved unable to engage the main British fortresses. When combined with the news of an Anglo-Indian assault on Mackinac Island, Hull decided to withdraw his army and fall back to the walls of Detroit. British general Isaac Brock followed closely behind Hull and soon approached the battlements of the fortified city. Employing stratagem rather than numbers, Brock was able to convince Hull of the hopelessness of his situation. In what became regarded as a national disgrace, Gen. Hull surrendered the city of Detroit to a much smaller British force on August 16.

The first loss of national territory since the British invasion of the southern colonies almost 30 years before was a major blow to American morale, fear of further attacks by the English and their Indian allies spread throughout the Northwest Territory. The elderly Robert Johnson expressed his thoughts to Pres. Madison that, "the Idea with us is, that Hull is a traitor or nearly an Ediot [sic] or part of both. To take a View of the whole of his Conduct, it would seem as if he has played the Grandest Yanke [sic] Trick that ever has been played on the U.S."[67]

Col. Richard Johnson was marching his men north when word reached them of the surrender of Detroit. Worse news was yet to come as a further series of villages and forts fell to the British and Indians over the next few weeks. One of these attacks was the infamous Fort Dearborn Massacre of August 15, 1812, which led to the death of over 50 men, women, and children. Tales of the brutality of the Natives spread through the region including the story of the valiant Capt. William

Wells whose heart was consumed by the Indians after they brought him down on the battlefield.[68] The logical next target for the enemy, Fort Wayne, stood exposed and dilapidated between the Wabash and Tippecanoe Rivers.

In early September an Indian force under Winamac approached the garrison, demanding its surrender. Captain James Rhea, weak and allegedly, "drunk as a fool all night," was lackluster in his commitment to defend the installation and was eventually removed from his post.[69] Reinforcements rushed to the area from surrounding states and territories, including Col. Johnson's mounted Kentuckians. By September 12th the siege was over and Maj. Gen. William Henry Harrison of Kentucky was able to enter the fort.

As part of Harrison's efforts to once again secure the region, small units were sent out to raid the surrounding area. One of these punitive chevauchées was conducted by the men under the command of Richard Mentor Johnson. Just days after arriving at Fort Wayne, Johnson and his men burned a series of Potawatomi villages along the Elkhart River, much as his father had done almost 30 years before. Located to the northwest of the recently relieved fortress, these villages represented a continuing threat to American settlement in the area. Their destruction would help to depopulate hostile Indians in the old northwest and secure the recapture of Detroit. Johnson explained his role in the war in a letter to Pres. Madison written on September 18, 1812, in which he extoled the virtue and martial powers of his men.

> "I have the honour of commanding the only Battalion of Mounted Riflemen now attached to the army at this place ... I have just returned from the Expedition to the Elkhart village upon the River of that name, which village we destroyed. Tomorrow we commence an expedition composed of mounted men, the object of which is to drive the Savages from our limits & distroy all we can find. We have considered the Miamies as enemies. The evidence of their hostility is complete ... I am at the head of the most choice men I have ever seen—who are now serving without pay & who volunteered

Knowing that pay was not authorised."[70]

Yet within a month of his successful raids, the Congressman was back in Washington DC, taking his appointed seat in the Capitol. His vote was needed on a number of bills to further the war, including taxation and the securing of loans. Yet his position as a War Hawk was always tempered by his western Democratic isolationism as seen during the debate over a proposal to increase the size of the navy that arose in December. Johnson argued against expanding the navy fearing that the acquisition of a large navy would lead America to foreign adventurism and more wars in the worst traditions of Rhodes, Crete, Athens, and Carthage. "Peace and tranquility is not the natural state of a great naval power."[71] Undoubtedly he also saw an increased focus on naval arms as a decreased focus on the current land war. In addition, he could not help but see the very concept of a navy as being part of the Federalist war against the poor and those of the interior.

> "While their commerce and navy furnished a small part of the people with the luxuries of every country at that time known, the great mass of citizens at home were miserable and oppressed, their rights neglected, their burdens increased, and their happiness destroyed, while their fleets and external grandeur carried astonishment and terror to distant nations. When a nation puts forth her strength upon the ocean, the interior of the country will be neglected and oppressed with contributions. Ancient history does not furnish a solitary instance of any permanent good or long continuance of peace arising from a great naval supremacy; such overgrown power, such unnatural strength, must feed upon plunder at home and abroad."[72]

With the American Revolution as a model for a successful war fought by a nation lacking a navy, Johnson argued that ...

> "But, I am asked, how will you contend with a maritime nation without a navy? Sir, that question is as easily answered as the first. I will ask how we succeeded in the Revolutionary War? We were without any se-

curity upon our seacoast and still we succeeded. But, to be more specific, I would grant letters of marque and reprisal, and authorize privateering. Give scope to individual enterprise to destroy the commerce of the enemy--which can be done effectually. I would fortify our seaport towns; station our gunboats and frigates along our coast to protect us at home. And, in this way, I would in war avenge the infractions of our neutral rights."[73]

At the same time, Johnson's knowledge and practice of Indian tactics pushed him to develop a new strategy for the war out west that he proposed to the President in December 1812. The idea called for the raising of units of mounted riflemen, much like the ones he had commanded on the Elkhart. These troops would transverse the Northwest Territory, raiding various Indian villages during the winter. These attacks would compel the Natives to stay close to their homes to defend their families, thus preventing raids against American frontier posts and towns.

> "The force here contemplated will be valuable if raised, not a minute ought to be lost. The proposition for this campaign has made the West rejoice. They expect something to be done. If the deposits should not be used by the mounted men, other troops will use them. The plan here presented in so many forms may be too complex and too expensive. It may be simplified in several particulars & perhaps it would be as well ... If successful how much more usefull than to keep troops inactive upon the frontiers."[74]

With two regiments of 640 men each raised in Kentucky, Johnson proposed an expedition be launched from Fort Wayne towards Illinois. His men would travel to the upper end of Lake Michigan, cross the Illinois River, and return to Louisville on the Ohio. Ravaging the region in coordination with a "large, bullet-proof boat," he hoped to clear the northwest area of enemy activity. In this proposal, he was seconded by his fellow War Hawk Henry Clay, who wrote Monroe in December

1812, "Of the Campaign proposed by Mr. Johnson I would say, that, considered in reference to a re-inforcement of Genl. Harrison, upon the experation of the term of service of the forces now under his command, it does appear to me entitled to encouragement."[75]

A few days before the close of Congress in February 1813, the Secretary of War wrote Johnson, encouraging him to, "organize and hold in readiness a Regiment of Mounted Volunteers."[76] Despite some resistance within his home state to this perhaps unconstitutional, unwise, or unethical raising of a state regiment by such a young congressman, he was quickly able to raise 1,000 men back in Kentucky in only a few days.[77] Unfortunately though, it was already too late in the year to undertake his strategy of winter warfare. This was perhaps for the best as Gen. Harrison himself considered the idea of a winter raid to be, "impractical to the extent proposed."[78] The general did, however, approve of its usage should it be undertaken in the summer or fall. Perhaps the greatest testament to the tactical soundness of Johnson's plan was the fact that the U.S. Army was still using it as a method to fight Indians out west in the 1880s.

Johnson canvassed Kentucky with fliers seeking to rouse the men of the state to join his unit to prosecute the war.

> "That crisis has arrived! Fort Meigs is attacked—the North-Western army is surrounded by the enemy, and under the command of General Harrison, nobly defending the sacred cause of their country, against a combined enemy, the British and Indians. They will maintain the ground until relieved. The intermediate garrisons are also in imminent danger, and may fall a bleeding sacrifice to savage fury, unless timely reinforced. The frontiers may also be deluged in blood; the Mounted Regiment will present a shield to the defenceless [sic], and united with forces marching ... the enemy will be driven from our soil."[79]

Image 2. Johnson at the Head of his Kentucky Mounted Rifles

Once his army was raised, Johnson set about training, disciplining, and supplying the men, arming his mounted soldiers with rifles, tomahawks, and knives. To make sure that all possible needs would be met while out on campaign, the Colonel also personally paid for the hiring of a blacksmith, a gunsmith, and doctors. Richard's older brother, Major James Johnson, worked to drill the cavalry force in charging the massed infantry lines of the British, a decision that was to pay dividends months later at the Battle of the Thames.[80] While his men were sharpening their martial skills, Johnson set about augmenting his own mental acumen by devouring whatever books on the art of war that he could lay his hands upon. He at one point even wrote in a letter to Thomas Jefferson that, "Every moment of Leisure since has been devoted to the Study of the various Branches of military Science including military history—I find my want of experience some disadvantage—but I have purchased every military Book in my reach." Later in the same letter, he asked the former President to, "add something by way of advice as to the manner of reading & the Books to read, particularly as it respects military history."[81]

Beginning in May 1813, Col. Richard Johnson and his brother James, who had recently been made a Lt. Col., began to raid Indian villages north of the Ohio River. Yet just as they had begun their bloody task news arrived of the dangerous situation confronting Ft. Meigs. Located at modern day Perrysburg, Ohio the fort had been constructed by Harrison beginning in January 1813 to provide a base for his campaign to retake Detroit. Issues of supply, the weather, and the expiration of enlistments for many of the militia dealt a blow to the general's plans for a spring offensive. Instead, as Harrison rushed to finish the fortification an English and Indian force landed at the Maumee River under Henry Proctor and Tecumseh. The siege of the fort was to last for over a week and would ultimately see the death or capture of almost 700 Americans, most of whom were fellow Kentuckians.

> "Fort Meigs is threatened with an attack by a force which it cannot resist. We will fly to its relief. The only ground in its vicinity which will answer for an encampment we shall probably find in the occupancy of a superior number of the enemy; and we shall no alternative but victory or death. If there be a man among us who is not fully resolved on this alternative, he has liberty to retire from the regiment. The tide of war must now be turned upon the foe; and Kentucky shall no longer mourn the fall of her gallant sons, but in the arms of victory."[82]

Johnson's men responded eagerly and patriotically to his call to arms. According to a later biographer, the mounted Kentucky regiment marched 50 miles in one day in an attempt to relieve the fort. Yet Proctor abandoned the attack on May 9, unable to reduce Harrison's fort. In fact another Kentucky force had arrived shortly before the siege and helped to repel the numerous assaults. One of the officers in this brigade was Richard's brother, Col. William Judah Johnson. Unfortunately though, he would ultimately be stricken with disease from the campaign, returning home to die in Kentucky in April 1814. Left behind were his young widow and a son, George Washington Johnson, who would grow up to be the first Confederate governor of Kentucky. William's son would likewise lose his own life in battle, in his case at Shiloh. Another brother, John Telemachus Johnson, served as Harrison's aide during the siege. He appears to have been actively involved in the battle, having had a horse shot out from under him during the engagement. John would also fall ill and return to Kentucky, sitting out the remainder of the war.

  Col. Johnson's men were approaching the town of Newport across from Cincinnati when they heard the news of the fort's salvation via a message from Harrison. The general thanked them for their service and suggested that these brave soldiers should disband and return home as danger no longer loomed on the horizon.[83] Harrison was at least in part still angry over the performance of the Kentuckians in his force whose brazen actions led to such a loss of life during the battle. Eager for glory and revenge however, Johnson and his men pushed forward, meeting up with Harrison and receiving permission to join the regular forces for their campaign against Detroit.

The success of American forces in the west owed itself largely to the generalship of William Henry Harrison, the hero of Tippecanoe. Johnson in fact was one of the loudest voices requesting the appointment of the Governor of Indiana Territory, and his future political opponent, to the post of commanding general. In a letter that he wrote to Pres. Madison in September 1812, Johnson stated that ...

> "I have been present with the army & have been a Strict observer of men & things and let me inform you that no event is now so important to the cause of our Country in this quarter as the giving Gov. Harrison the command of the forces from Kentucky destined for Canada. He has capacity without an equal. He has the confidence of the forces without a parrellel in our History except in the case of Genl. Washington in the revolution."[84]

He wrote in a similar vein to former President Thomas Jefferson on February 9, 1813. "It is my opinion that the materials of the North W. Army (with whom I served 50 days) are equal to the best army in Europe & that they would at this moment act as worthy under the Gallant Commander Gen. Harrison as did the Athenean militia at Marathon."[85] This endorsement was likewise echoed by his father who also wrote the President in September 1812 declaring that, "the men have great Confidence in Harrison."[86] This praise of Harrison would come back to haunt the younger Johnson when the two sparred off as opponents in the Election of 1840.

William Henry Harrison formalized a plan to assault Detroit by land and sea before crossing the border and taking the fight directly to southwestern Ontario. Col. Johnson and his mounted regiment continued to raid through Indian territory before finally rendezvousing with Harrison at Ft. Winchester (Defiance, Oh.) on June 18, 1813. The Kentuckians lived in perpetual fear of attack by the natives of the region and formed a secure square camp every night which had cannon taken from Ft. Meigs positioned at its four corners. Johnson continued to engage and battle the various tribal forces of the region while waiting for the hoped for campaign against Detroit and Canada.

Yet his hopes were momentarily dashed when in June 1813 a letter arrived from the new secretary of war, John Armstrong. In an effort to protect the Illinois frontier against a feared Indian incursion, the President had ordered that various mounted units, including Johnson's, to be dispatched to Kaskaskia on the Mississippi. The site of George Rogers Clark's famed Revolutionary victory was to serve as a forward post for responding to any attacks by the Native allies of the British. Johnson was indignant at the order and quickly penned a communique to General Harrison. In the letter dated July 9, Col. Johnson informs his commander that the relocation to Kaskaskia would be ill advised due to both the approaching expiration of his men's enlistments as well as the lack of a credible Indian threat to the western Illinois border. Instead he asks to be allowed to stay near Lake Erie in order to continue to protect the region.[87] Though Johnson was most likely simply desirous of being a part of the upcoming campaign against Detroit rather than being assigned patrol duty at the edge of American civilization, his argument was helped by contemporary events.

On July 7, 1813, Dick Johnson with around 800 men of his mounted regiment were accompanying a supply convoy to Fort Wayne. As they approached, a group of Indians viciously attacked the supply boats, killing three men. Though the Kentuckians pursued the attackers they were unable to catch them. In retaliation Johnson proceeded to launch a series of punitive raids against villages of the area but achieved little strategic benefit by this. A variety of factors eventually compelled Johnson to escort the remaining ships home while a large party of Natives moved north through the unburned villages to join Tecumseh at Detroit.

Though still in disagreement with the orders from the War Department to proceed to the west, Johnson nonetheless loyally began to march his 800 men towards Kaskaskia. On July 14 while on the road to Piqua, Johnson penned a letter to President Madison in which he expressed his doubts about the assignment but still stated his willingness to follow the order.

> "I am happy to inform you, that we are attempting to execute your order with dispatch & from the great personal sacrifices the wealthy of the Regt are making to get horses for the dismounted & from other arrangements I am animated with a hope that we shall carry to Kaskaskias about 800 efficient men— ... And altho we left the N. W. Army with some reluctance owing to considerations urged in my letter to Genl. Harrison who promised to transmit a copy to you, I now feel perfectly satisfied & happy in the order, which we recd. to march to the Mississippi."[88]

His intended route called for an advance from the mouth of the Huron River in Ohio southwest to Piqua, from there he would traverse Indiana to reach Vincennes on the Wabash River, and finally use the river and trails to reach Kaskaskia.

Luckily for Johnson, planners in Washington realized the folly of dispatching so many mounted riflemen to the western hinterlands far from the main theater of battle. Secretary Armstrong in response sent a letter dated July 14, 1813, requesting the return of the various units to Harrison's command if at all possible. The general wrote back nine days later saying that he had, "sent after Colo. Johnson—*he* may be overtaken at Urbana, but the greater part of his men have scattered and gone off to Ky after fresh Horses."[89] Harrison's messenger did eventually catch up with Johnson near the latter's home by Great Crossings, Kentucky, apparently not in any rush to actually reach Kaskaskia. The Colonel assured Madison in a reply that his regiment, now resupplied, would be at Urbana shortly.[90] At the same time, Governor Shelby of Kentucky raised his own force of volunteers and likewise proceeded north to join the main army.

The campaign that was to make Richard Mentor Johnson a household name began in earnest in September 1813. With Perry's famed victory on Lake Erie, many of whose shipboard sharpshooters were drawn from Johnson's own regiment, the position of Proctor in Michigan became untenable.[91] Frightened by the exaggerated tales of Harrison's numbers, Proctor abandoned Detroit, razed Ft. Malden, and proceeded inland. Around two weeks after the engagement on Lake Erie, Harrison wrote to Johnson ordering him to move his force north to the River Raisin. On the 28th of that month Johnson and his men fulfilled their orders and secured the fallen village of Frenchtown in Michigan Territory. In the previous January over 500 men, mostly Kentuckians, had been killed by Proctor and his Indian allies in what became known as the River Raisin Massacre. The recapture of the city by sons of Kentucky must have been viewed with at least a modicum of restored pride by survivors of the original slaughter. Yet the sight of the ruined settlement, the unburied bodies, and the disinterred remains only served to spread rage through the army. Johnson himself would state years later that, "I never thirsted for a man's blood, but Proctor was a monster. Even Tecumseh ... was shocked at the conduct of the cowardly assassin."[92]

Col. Johnson quickened his pace and by September 30 he entered Detroit, just a few days behind Harrison. According to state lore Harrison was reluctant to follow the British into Canada but was prompted to do so at the urgings of Shelby who insisted that they, "follow Proctor and his savages to Hell if necessary, to avenge the wrongs of Kentucky."[93] As the commanding general had already secured the town and that of Sandwich on the opposite bank of the river, the entrance of the Kentuckians into Detroit lacked any fanfare, pomp, or danger. After a hard ride, Johnson finally caught up to the main army under Gen. Harrison on October 2, 1813, in Canada; the American invasion could now commence.

The Army of the Northwest was a collection of regulars and militia, most of who were drawn from the state of Kentucky. The infantry were composed of 120 men from the 27ᵗʰ U.S. Regiment as well as 2,380 militiamen under the direct command of Gov. Isaac Shelby of the Blue Grass State. Attached to this force as well now stood the 1,000 mounted riflemen of Col. Johnson. These were battle-hardened men, many of whom had suffered personal loss due to British and Indian deprivation in the region. Opposed to the American force stood Proctor's British army which consisted of perhaps 800 men and 500 Native allies under the legendary warrior Tecumseh.

The American army drew ever closer to the British force as it advanced through southwestern Ontario. By the night of October 3, Johnson's men were able to skirmish with some Indians from Proctor's rearguard. At one point a sniper's bullet even felled a man to the back of Johnson as the Kentuckians were watering their horses. All along the way the Americans found deserters, stragglers, abandoned ordinance, and equipment and buildings that had been hastily set alight. Though the enemy attempted to slow their pursuers by destroying bridges, the mounted regiment helped to ferry the army across a fordable part of the Thames River, each horseman taking a soldier, allowing for the famed engagement that was to follow on October 5, 1813.

The Battle of the Thames was as important for America's future in the old northwest as it was for the personal future of Richard Mentor Johnson. The Congressman was a few miles ahead of the main force, gathering information on the British position through personal observation and the capture of a few enemy combatants. Harrison had ordered him to pursue the retreating foe with his force, urging him, "if you cannot compel them to stop without an engagement, why fight them, but do not venture too much."[94] Thanks to his intelligence gathering it soon became apparent that Proctor had organized his force into two lines separated in the middle by a small swamp. His flanks were anchored on the left by the Thames and on the right by more swampland as he straddled the peninsula between Lake St. Clair and Lake Ontario. Additional Indians were positioned in a mass in the swamp on the right amidst a tangle of trees and undergrowth.

When Harrison rode up to confirm with Johnson about the upcoming battle, the General had originally intended for Johnson to charge the

Indians on the left while he engaged the British on the right with the infantry. Yet after examining the terrain the Colonel discovered that the swampy ground imperiled his force, making a direct assault impossible. Harrison responded by ordering Johnson to withdraw with his men and act as a mobile reserve, a suggestion that the Kentuckian, eager for action, quickly rejected. Johnson instead suggested that his men be allowed to charge the enemy troops. "General Harrison, permit me to charge the enemy and the battle shall be won in thirty minutes."[95] Proctor had left his men in an open order with at several feet of space between each man.[96] The months of training that James Johnson had given his men in confronting ranks of infantry had prepared them for this exact scenario. The Colonel told Harrison that his men were ready to charge with an "Indian yell" and with bayonets armed. Two equal columns of mounted riflemen would descend upon the divided British; one under James Johnson and the other under his brother Richard. Their target was to be the British left under Proctor which was anchored on the Thames. Once this unit was defeated, if the Indians did not subsequently flee, Richard Mentor Johnson could then lead his men across the swamp to engage the larger enemy right under Tecumseh. By dividing his forces on either side of the swamp, Proctor had effectively nullified his chances of using his wings to support each other. William Henry Harrison approved of the suggestion, exclaiming, "damn them, charge them," and returned to command the militia for the follow up attack once the British line was broken.[97] Johnson confirmed his role as the organizer of the American victory years later in a letter to General Armstrong, "It is due to truth to state that I requested General Harrison to permit me to charge, and, knowing that I had trained my men for it, during our short service, he gave me the order."[98] As the two brothers began to prepare for battle a scout arrived to inform the Colonel of a path across the swamp. Richard Johnson quickly formulated a new strategy, giving command of the main force to his brother to engage Proctor, while he himself would lead the secondary force against Tecumseh. Exclaiming to his brother that, "you have a family, I have none," Richard volunteered himself for the more dangerous portion of the battlefield.[99] The larger strategy here was to eliminate both the British and Indian threats in one fell swoop rather than allowing one or the other unit to disengage and withdrew further into the wilderness of Upper Canada with the winter quickly approaching.

Exactly 8 months and 13 days after the River Raisin Massacre, Johnson's men charged to the sound of a bugle blaring. The Kentuckians let out the cry, "Remember the Raisin and Revenge," and hurled themselves at the British left under Proctor's direct command.[100] The English were so unprepared that their opening volley injured only one horse among the charging Americans.[101] James Johnson's assault was an unprecedented success as he broke through the English ranks and then doubled back to encircle the startled enemy. With only one American casualty to speak of the entire British line crumbled and Proctor fled the field of battle. Yet the American left under Richard Mentor Johnson was to witness a much fiercer assault.

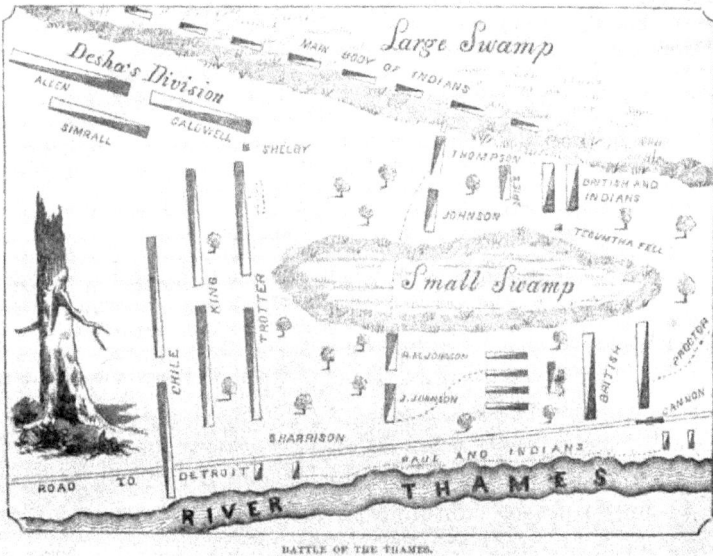

Image 3. The Battle of the Thames

With Proctor defeated, Col. Johnson led a forlorn hope of 20 men across the small swamp and towards Tecumseh's men. As he recounted years later at a campaign rally, "having promised the wives, mothers, and sister of my men before we left Kentucky that I would place their

46

husbands, sons, and brothers in no hazard which I was unwilling to share myself, I put myself at the head of these twenty men."[102] According to a later campaign biographer one of the men in the group was 70-year-old Col. Whitley who had served previously in the Revolution. While some claim that this aged veteran issued the order, "let our watchword this day be victory or death," and was instantly shot dead, others contend that he perished during the battle, and still others that he was the man who killed Tecumseh.[103] In sharp contrast to the action on the British left, the murderous fire of the Indians quickly dropped 15 of Johnson's men. The small swamp between the two forces and accurate gunfire of the enemy held up Johnson's advance and forced him to abandon his plan to undertake a suicide charge in order to provide an opening for the main American force. Instead, having drawn the attention of the Indians he ordered his entire regiment of 500 men to move forward. As his horsemen were having trouble with their footing in the dismal swamp, he ordered the whole force to dismount save for himself who sat proudly upon a white charger.

Though outnumbered two-to-one, the Kentuckians bravely slogged through the mud, debris, and shattered bodies. Col. Johnson, conspicuous atop his mount, was wounded four times, with his horse being perhaps the only thing holding him upright. It is at this point that eyewitness accounts mix with legends and campaign literature to paint a picture of what occurred next. Amidst the roar of battle the wounded Johnson spotted an Indian chief, richly adorned with his face covered in black and red lines according to some, clad only in a deer buckskin to others. Convinced that this Native was Tecumseh, or at least an important commander, Johnson spurred his horse onwards towards him. Yet in an almost comic action, as the Colonel's horse rounded a tree it tripped and fell on an exposed root; certainly the 15 bullets discovered in the horse later didn't improve its stability any. Though he was not seriously injured by the accident, he lost the element of surprise. Alerted to the presence of this lone rider, Tecumseh leveled his rifle and shot. The bullet struck Johnson, hitting the upper joint of his finger and continuing onward before passing through his wrist. The Indian chief then dropped his gun and gripped his tomahawk, charging at the wounded American. Col. Johnson calmly drew his own pistol and shot Tecumseh in the chest, felling the great warrior. According to oral traditions at the time, Tecumseh had a premonition of his own death in battle that day and had given away his possessions and shaken the hands of the British officers before leading his men forward.[104]

The death of Tecumseh caused the entire Indian line to eventually crumble. After little more than 15 minutes of battle, screaming and wailing warriors fled the battlefield in a disorganized rout, loudly lamenting the loss of their leader. According to his campaign biography the badly wounded Johnson exclaimed after the killing, "the victory is ours, make the best of it."[105] Still others that he turned to a trusted aide and exclaimed, "I will not die. I am mightily cut to pieces, but I think my vitals have escaped."[106] A fellow Kentuckian later described Johnson as serene in his agony and resigned to his noble fate.[107] He then fainted from loss of blood and had to be carried from the battlefield. Perhaps the true testament to his bravery in battle was the fact that his wounded horse also collapsed into unconsciousness before dying a few minutes later, having suffered as many injuries as its rider. Upon examination, it was claimed, Johnson's coat held 25 bullets imbedded within it, five of which had directly injured him, most notably in the hip and thigh. As Gen. Harrison himself opined, "his numerous wounds proved his was the post of danger."[108]

Image 4. Johnson Kills Tecumseh

Though in the end the fight lasted only 18 minutes and yielded no more than 60 casualties for the Americans and perhaps 240 for the British and Indians, it was an immense victory for the United States. Tecumseh was dead and with him the hopes of an Indian confederation in the northwest. The Americans were once again firmly in possession of Michigan and even had a foothold in Canada. In addition, coming as it did amidst the general stalemate in the New York theater of war, the battle helped to raise American morale and relieve pressure on Madison to supply a major victory in the war. According to Richard Rush the President was overjoyed by the news, "the little President is back, and as game as ever."[109] It is little wonder that the battle was celebrated for years afterwards and was once described by a notable Kentucky historian as the most "Norman" of American victories.[110]

Many doubted at the time and afterwards that Johnson was actually the man who had killed Tecumseh. As he himself famously said, "I didn't stop to ask him his name."[111] A brief review of some of the evidence presented by his contemporaries would be appropriate here. Most notable perhaps were the eyewitness accounts of such trusted persons as legendary Indian fighter Anthony Shane as well as the forensic evidence that Tecumseh had been hit by two buckshots and a ball from above, the exact same load that the mounted Richard Mentor Johnson typically fired.[112] Chief Shaw-ben-eh, who had been present on the field with Tecumseh, described years later how the great warrior, already wounded, decided to charge at Johnson in hopes of being killed by a great enemy rather than an ordinary soldier.[113] In addition, while some Natives suggested that his body had been removed from the battlefield or left to rot and be eaten by wild animals, others contend that it is more likely that the Indian leader was scalped and skinned by American soldiers the next day as were numerous others.[114] Terrance Kirby of Kentucky confirmed this much in a letter years later to Pres. Abraham Lincoln. "I [helped] kill Tecumseh and [helped] skin him, an brot Two pieces of his yellow hide home with me to my Mother & Sweet Hart.[115] Johnson and his men also had the good luck to recapture the Burgoyne Cannon, a gun allegedly acquired at the Battle of Saratoga in 1777, lost after the fall of Detroit, and now retaken by the Kentuckians who brought it back to Frankfort where it remains today.[116] Johnson himself focused for years afterwards on the victory rather than the victim, and in the end this was the more notable accomplishment.

Johnson's regiment would go on to raid the nearby settlement of Mora-viantown before withdrawing back to Detroit before the onset of cold-er weather. The Colonel himself returned to Detroit earlier than his unit and spent almost two weeks in recovering. Gen. Harrison in his first official dispatch to the President written shortly after the battle in fact gave the wounding of Johnson prominent attention.

> "I have the honor to inform you, that by the blessing of Providence, the army under my command has this eve-ning obtained a complete victory over the combined Indian and British forces under the command of Proc-tor. I believe that nearly the whole of the enemy's regu-lars are taken or killed. Amongst the former are all the superior officers excepting gen. Proctor. My mounted men are now in pursuit of him. Our loss is very trifling. The brave col. R. M. Johnson is the only officer whom I have heard of that is wounded, he badly, but I hope not dangerously."[117]

The swelling of his hand led doctors to seriously consider amputation in order to save his life. Though Johnson "bravely" refused to have his hand removed and did eventually recover, he was permanently left with a crippled appendage.[118] This war wound would go on to serve him well during future campaign rallies, as tangible evidence of his nationalism and accomplishment. Once the danger of death had passed, Johnson was conveyed by litter through driving November rains for hundreds of miles. His elderly father ventured as far as Ohio to retrieve his son and the two were back in Kentucky by late November. Yet though his body was crippled his indomitable spirit still evoked awe from those around him.

Awards and accolades were showered upon the slayer of Tecumseh. His fellow War Hawk and Kentuckian Henry Clay praised him on the floor of Congress noting that he was one of the few Congressmen who "exhibited the more than Roman example in shouldering their mus-kets and flying to the protection of the frontiers, against a most sav-age alliance."[119] According to tradition, he turned down all prizes from

Congress until Gen. Harrison received a gold medal. The latter had been relegated to a secondary theater by Sec. of War Armstrong shortly after the victory and had resigned in disgust, with the magnitude of his victories not being recognized for years. While in Johnson's home state, the ladies of Scott County awarded him with a ceremonial sword. The saber was officially presented to him by the 80-year-old mother of one of the casualties of the battle. Additionally, Johnson received an iron tomahawk from Lt. H.H. Rhodes who served aboard Perry's flagship and shortly afterwards Gen. Alexander McComb, the hero of Plattsburgh, likewise gave him a sword in recognition of his actions, allegedly a blade that had belonged to the Duke of Suffolk, who had been executed for rebellion in 1554.[120] In December 1813, while he was still recovering from his wounds, the city of Lexington held a public dinner at which 25 toasts were drank in the Colonel's honor.[121] Nor was Johnson the only one to benefit from the campaign. In all nine Kentuckians present at the Battle of the Thames would go on to secure office as governors, senators, representatives, or lieutenant governors.

Though most likely still in pain and allegedly unable to walk well, Richard Mentor Johnson was back in his Congressional seat in February 1814. He was initially tasked by Pres. Madison, along with Sen. Jeremiah Morrow of Ohio, to negotiate peace with the Northwest Indians. Yet as both were Congressmen at the time it was soon deemed to be a conflict of interests and they were instead replaced by Gen. Harrison. That year proved to be one of the most potentially disastrous for the Union as three British armies converged on the eastern seaboard. One of these axes of advances was aimed at the port city of Baltimore. When the English assault against the famed Fort McHenry failed the army instead turned to vent its wrath on the young city of Washington. In the last week of August 1814 troops under Robert Ross proceeded to burn the fledgling America capital to the ground. The majority of public buildings were reduced to ashes, including the White House and Capitol, and President Madison and members of the government who were in the capital fled to Brookeville, Maryland.

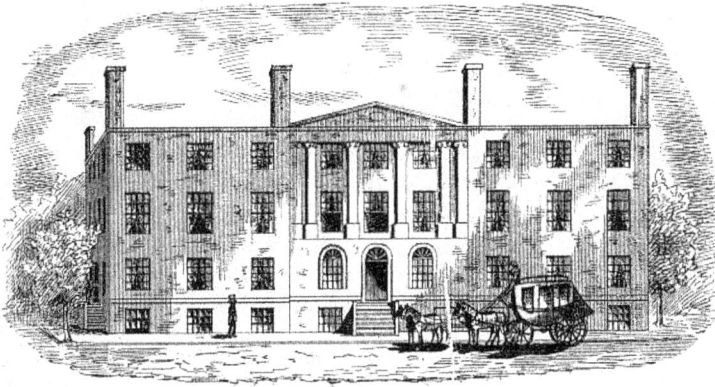

Image 5. The Bloodgett Hotel

Yet as quickly as the English arrived they left, as their failure to reduce Ft. McHenry endangered their presence in the region. When the President issued a call for Congress to assemble at the capital only a few weeks later, Johnson responded and the wounded warrior rejoined his fellow legislators at Blodget's Hotel in Washington. Many spoke out for the permanent relocation of the nation's capital further inland or back to Philadelphia to avoid a repetition of what had occurred in the future. Yet many other voices, including that of Johnson, opposed the action and argued against it. As Johnson eloquently expressed, "we ought not to yield a triumph which the enemy never claimed."[122] In the end, Congress turned down the mostly northern measure in October 1814 by a vote of 83-74.

Instead the young Congressman and war hero felt that the nation would be better served by the formation of a committee to investigate the causes of the fall of Washington. On September 22nd, only a few weeks after the burning of Washington, Johnson stood before Congress to recommend the creation of such a body.[123] His fellow legislators approved of the recommendation and Johnson himself was named as chairman. Its charge, as laid out in a letter from Secretary of the Navy William Jones to Johnson in October 1814, was, "to enquire into the causes of the success of the enemy in his enterprises against this Metropolis, and the neighbouring town of Alexandria, and into the manner in which the Public buildings and property were destroyed, and the amount thereof."[124] Though the committee's work was completed by November and its information released to the public, it declined to issue an opinion or to find fault.

The same year that Johnson was wrapping up his investigation into the burning of the capital, the Kentuckian ran unopposed for his Congressional seat in the third district and was returned to Washington. He allegedly set about formulating a plan for yet another invasion of Canada for the start of the 1815 campaign season. However, before he could bring his plans to fruition, word arrived in Washington of the peace settlement at Ghent that effectively ended the War of 1812.

Yet Johnson's concern for the nation and those who had fought for her did not ebb with the cessation of hostilities. The rather large number of men who still remained under arms in defense of the young country were running short of food, pay, and supplies. Representative Johnson, having himself experienced privation in the field, became an early vocal supporter of their cause. Writing President Madison in June 1815, only months after the ending of hostilities, Johnson explained the issue confronting the army.

> "If my conduct for seven years past & which has come under your notice has any claims upon you I solicit the perusal of the above mentioned letters & extend such relief as may be in your power; It appears as if the funds for Supplying the troops of the U.S. are exhausted. Of Course other funds must be transfered to this object or the army must Starve & contractors ruined; or the Army of the U. S. for 8 months to come must depend for food upon private resources ... I Know the Secy of the Treasury has the power to issue Treasury Notes. I also know that the President has the power to transfer appropriations. These considerations give me hope ... If aid Should be extended it is not for profit, or private purposes, but for the discharge of debts due & becoming due for feeding the army; to men who have furnishd flour, whiskey beef &c &c &c.

Give this aid, & as the army is reduced the Contractors will hereafter be enabled to feed the force in their district untill Congress shall Meet. I am truely Sorry, Sir, that the necessity of the Case has compelled me to trouble you, on this occasion, but in such a case to whom can we appeal? To this man who has our confidence & the power & whose administration has been as glorious and as brilleant as his Services have been conspicuous & his virtues acknowledged; and if these men are to be ruined & credit Sunk what other injury can be inflicted upon them Nothing can be more Severe."[125]

In a similar vein Johnson again wrote the President later that month seeking payment for additional vendors. This time he mentioned one firm in particular, Ward & Taylor of Philadelphia. Johnson's concern though was far from altruistic as one of the partners in the company was James Johnson, the Congressman's brother. "Without some aid Ward & Taylor & their partner James Johnson must be ruined before congress convenes, & that they ask only for money to pay the debts contracted in the Winter & Spring to feed the army under the Command of Genl. Jackson."[126] His brother also wrote the President as well as General Jackson, again detailing how he did, "supply that vallient army as well as any army was ever supply."[127] Yet before we cast too harsh a light on the motives of Johnson he reminds us later in the same letter that without the efforts of investors like his brother who invested their treasure as the soldiers did their lives, the war would have been lost. "Now it appears that the army is to be paid who fought so gallantly & that the Contractors & their friends their securities are to be plunged into utter ruin for the want of 200,000 dollars; Every cent of which was incurred to feed that very army, without the interposition of the President of the U. States."[128] A few years later during a debate with Federalist and anti-war Congressman Cyrus King, Johnson blamed most of the financial problems and disasters associated with the war as stemming from, "this mean, submitting spirit, united to an incessant opposition to the Administration, the object of which was power."[129]

Several additional military related issues arose in connection with the war. One of these was what to do with the standing army once the fighting was done. There was to be a similar discussion at the end of most major conflicts in American history stretching up to the ending of the Cold War. Viewpoints ranged from the extremes of the nation maintaining a large permanent force to a return to state militias. Richard Mentor Johnson spoke out in favor of reducing the regular army to only 6,000 men, the smallest number proposed. His thinking in this was directly in line with Thomas Jefferson's own views when the latter took office over a decade before. In fact many of the founding fathers were vehemently opposed to the notion of a standing army, seeing it as a tool of tyranny. After much heated debate, Congress eventually compromised on a force of 10,000 to protect the expanding nation for years to come. Much as with the case of ancient Rome, it was not to be on the backs of soldiers that the state prospered but of men and morals of olden times, men such as Richard Mentor Johnson.

A second issue concerned the establishment of military academies on the model of West Point. Johnson proposed in December 1815 that Congress appropriate money for three martial schools. Not surprisingly one of them was to be located at Newport, Kentucky with the others in South Carolina and Washington DC. While local jealousies soon prompted Congressmen to appeal for the schools to be in their own states or for simply one national academy to be funded in the capital, Johnson argued along the lines of sectionalism. He feared that a national school would soon become stocked with children of the capital's elite while regional schools would better attract local talent. In this he was supported by Henry Clay, John C. Calhoun, and others. Ultimately though, lack of a general consensus ultimately led to the bill being tabled by 1816. Johnson did continue to push for various armories to be established, "on the western waters," throughout his time in Congress to both bring protection and patronage to the trans-Mississippian United States.[130]

A third concern was the nonexistent transportation system by which to move men and material across the country in times of war. The dearth of an organized road system had been clearly laid bare by the war. The concept of investing in such a network thus appealed to not only those patriots concerned with the military safety of their nation, but to industrialists and westerners as well. Johnson as a combination of all three types therefore became an early advocate of the idea. As early as February 22, 1816, he reported on behalf of the Committee on Military Affairs that, "it is expedient at this time to make additional provision by law for military transportation."[131] While in 1818, he voted in favor of the President employing active duty soldiers, "otherwise reposing in sloth, and contracting the vices of the camp," to construct roads and bridges.[132] The concept would make him at least initially an advocate of Clay's American System.

Finally, as chair of the Military Committee, Richard Johnson sought a solution to the problems that arose with the militia during the early years of the war. Militia from New York had infamously refused to cross over the border into Canada in support of Stephen van Rensselaer's offensive in 1812. This, when combined with other factors, led to that officers defeat at Queenston Heights in the first major battle of the war. Likewise, several New England governors had refused to allow their militia to be used by the President for the purposes of campaigns outside the country. Johnson's bill requested the Secretary of War to submit a plan for, "a system for the organization and discipline of the militia, best calculated, in his opinion, to promote the efficiency of that force, when called into the public service."[133] Yet Congress could not agree to a method by which to force governors to comply with a presidential request for soldiers and the matter ultimately went nowhere.

Overall, the War of 1812 changed the course of both American history as well as the political career of Richard Mentor Johnson. The country had avenged its perceived wrongs at the hands of the British, the Indian threat in the old northwest had been eliminated bringing peace and safety to Kentucky and the other states of the region, and Johnson became a national hero. His *cognomina ex virtute* of the Hero of the Thames or the Slayer of Tecumseh would become the centerpiece of his various political campaigns. The anniversary of his great victory was celebrated almost annually near his farm in Kentucky with toasts given to the soldiers, Shelby, Waitly, and most importantly Johnson. It was remembered as the triumph of western, agrarian volunteers over the aristocratic, British regulars a foil for the political battles between the Democratic Party and their Federalist/Whig rivals.

CHAPTER IV

FROM THE HOUSE TO THE SENATE AND BACK AGAIN

Richard Mentor Johnson was a rising star in the House in the years immediately following the War of 1812. Known historically as the Era of Good Feelings, the decade from 1815 to 1825 witnessed relative economic prosperity, peace abroad, and the advent of a one party system within the nation. Though the country as a whole may have prospered and moved forward, many segments of society failed to advance. The Congressman from Kentucky once again emerged as a partisan supporter of the poor and infirm, using his influence and office to secure legislation for the less fortunate of both his state and the nation.

In this way, Johnson was evolving politically in a similar way to many of his fellow Republicans. The party of limited government, states' rights, and concern for individual freedom and liberty was slowly becoming the Democratic Party of the modern era. Expanded suffrage and the growth of industrialization and urbanization meant that government was being expected to intervene and solve more problems in the lives of its citizens. Men like Dick Johnson who were historically champions of the common man adhered easily to this new philosophy. He consistently saw his enemies as new incarnations of the Federalists, once describing them to Jefferson as, "Tories, British, Heretings [sic], Aristocrats, Monarchists, & the political apostates."[134] He was the champion of the young, western debtor against the established, eastern aristocrat. In many ways he continued to fight the socioeconomic equivalency of the War of 1812 during his many years in the legislature.

In the years immediately after the Treaty of Ghent, Johnson took up the standard of those who were widowed, orphaned, or wounded due to the conflict. Speech after speech was given on the floor of the House pleading upon the behalf of those who had served in either the Revolution or the War of 1812. Johnson considered the money owed to them to be a debt of gratitude on behalf of the country rather than a mere handout. So eloquently did he and others orate that Congress approved a number of pensions and programs. One representative at the time exclaimed following one of Richard Johnson's discourses, "that speech will cost the nation a million of dollars."[135] A further contemporary summarized Johnson's accomplishments in this arena as ...

> "Of all measures which were adopted by congress to provide for the fatherless and widows of those who had fallen in their country's service, he was either the projector or the firm supporter. And, we may add, that more honour redounds to the country from these acts, than from all the victories achieved by our prowess."[136]

Yet he did not confine himself to helping simply the women and children affected by the war. Captivity narratives had arisen in American literature as a popular native art form in the seventeenth century. The constant presence of savage Natives just beyond the pale of civilization waiting to kidnap young women and enslave men became engrained in the American psyche. Johnson, as a product of such an environment in early Kentucky, as well as a loyal comrade in arms, became concerned with the fate of captured and missing Americans after the ending of the war. In an effort not seen again until perhaps the conflict in Vietnam, Congressmen such as Johnson used their offices to investigate tales of prisoners of war still being held by the Indians years after the Treaty of Ghent.

Numerous letters exist written by Johnson concerning still captive Americans. One such communique appearing in the *Argus* on January 29, 1817, verifies Johnson's broaching of the topic with the highest levels of the government.

> "We have received information from several gentlemen in Kentucky, that one of our citizen soldiers has lately returned from Indian captivity, and has given information that a number of our fellow-citizens remain behind in the same situation, captive to the Indians, and that our neighbor Fant, the musician, was near Quebec held as the property of an Indian in the British service, as a musician. I have seen the president and the secretary and most of the members from Kentucky, who

have taken an interest in this thing ... the president will employ a special messenger to traverse the wilderness and search after those unfortunate captives who are deprived of liberty, by risking their lives in defense of their country."[137]

A reply a few months later from Secretary of State Richard Rush showed that Johnson's concerns were being addressed by authorities on both sides of the border. "I have the honor to send you the copy of a letter from Mr. Bagot ... on the subject of certain American prisoners, who were supposed to be still held in captivity by the Indians upon Lake Huron, in whose cases you have taken so much interest."[138] Though Rush states that the Canadians have informed him that no Thomas Fant exists around Quebec, they do acknowledge that, "some individuals may possibly be yet in captivity in the neighborhood of Lake Huron (meaning, it is presumed, American citizens) and that he would avail himself of any information which might be communicated through this government, for the discovery of such, with a view to their release."[139]

Johnson also continued his efforts to obtain favors and positions for his friends, supporters, and constituents back in Kentucky as well. His enemies would continuously suggest some sort of corruption in the practice. James Taylor writing to President Madison in 1813 questioned the many appointments being made by Johnson. "Our friend Richard with all his good qualities is so fond of popularity that he regards that more than merit & has made some of the worst appointments in the State."[140] Johnson had to defend himself more than once to the press and presidents. As early as 1813 we find in a letter to Madison, "No man thank God will ever look me in the face & say I ever accepted of a cent for corrupt purposes!"[141] Johnson was merely a product of his time and a believer in the Democratic spoils system made famous during the presidency of Andrew Jackson. Patronage was a way for the common man to ascend through the ranks, in addition it helped to spread political power, and join others to the system. To Jacksonian Democrats, patronage was democracy.

Though deeply partisan with regards to issues of poverty, Johnson was at the same time in tune with various bipartisan issues of the day. One of these was the topic of protective tariffs that accompanied the rise of industry in America. Concern over the inability of infant industries to thrive in a market dominated by the "Satanic mills" of England led economists and politicians from Alexander Hamilton to Henry Clay to argue for the placement of a tax on all goods coming into the country in order to make American products more competitive. The South had historically resented tariffs due to the higher costs that they forced upon the consumer, concerns over free trade, and a distaste for the negative elements of industrialization, thus making the issue anathema for many Republicans. Yet in the aftermath of the war, many patriotic members of the party were concerned about the weak state of American manufacturing should conflict once again resume. At the same time western members of the party saw it as a boon for fledgling domestic industry along the Ohio River. The three year Dallas Tariff was therefore seen by most of the War Hawks as a patriotic necessity, a bitter pill to swallow for a few short years. Johnson was naturally one of these many Congressmen who voted "yes." In a similar fashion, he proposed an amendment to a bill in January 1816 pushing for increased duties on white lead imported into the nation as this product was extensively mined around Lexington, Kentucky. Johnson's support for tariffs would continue well into the next decade with him voting for the controversial Tariff of 1824 and the 1828 Tariff of Abominations.

In keeping with these ideas, Johnson proposed a bill to Congress in December 1817 to further push American manufacturing. "That the committee of commerce and manufactures be instructed to enquire into the expediency of providing by law for clothing the army and navy of the United States exclusively in American manufactures."[142] He argued for this move on the grounds of national security. Yet to placate the concerns of free trading conservatives who feared that lack of foreign competition would lead to higher prices he assured his fellow Congress that, "competition of the manufacturers among themselves would be so great ... as to give the article to the government at the lowest possible price."[143]

"BONUS" BILL
FEBRUARY 8, 1817
Vote on Passage

Yeas   Nays
Not voting   Unsettled, etc.
Votes not shown=(general ticket): N. H., 1 yea;
N. J., 3 nays; Ga., 1 nay; (districts): Pa., 1
nay; Md., 1 nay

Image 6. The Voting on the Bonus Bill of 1817

An additional bipartisan attempt was made at using the proceeds from the Second Bank of the United States to fund internal improvements across the expanding nation. The vote on this Bonus Bill of 1817 proved to be very contentious in Congress with both New England and the South opposing it. Johnson, as a western legislator faced a political dilemma. On the one hand, he had historically been an opponent of the Bank as an institution, yet on the other he realized that internal improvements would most directly benefit the west. Richard Mentor Johnson was one of the votes eagerly sought by proponents of the law and in the end he cast his vote for the measure. In the end it managed to pass the House by a vote of 86 to 84. As such he was only one of two Kentucky congressmen to do so. When President Madison subsequently vetoed the legislation he eagerly joined the effort to override the chief executive's opposition. Though in the end this move by Congress failed, it once again represented the spirit of bipartisan, regional politics that had largely settled upon the nation. Many of these views and votes would come back to haunt Johnson in the future once the platform of the Jacksonian Democratic Party became solidly against such issues and ideas.

Perhaps his most controversial piece of legislation came in 1815 and threatened to derail yet another bid for re-election. Congress had now been in place for 27 years and yet during that time its members had received no raise or change in their compensation. Representatives were still earning a salary of $6 a day for times they were in session. In an average year this amounted to around $900, which meant that Congressmen were earning less than 28 of the clerks who worked for them.[144] In addition, many felt that sessions of Congress were being unnecessarily dragged out simply to get more pay for its members.

In response to these issues, Richard Mentor Johnson proposed a measure in December 1815 that would set Congressional salaries at $1,500 per year, "nothing extravagant, nothing abhorrent."[145] Not only would this represent a $600 raise above their current pay but he hoped it would encourage legislators to complete their work faster as now there was no reason to tarry in Washington any longer than was necessary.[146] Debate on the issue began on March 4, 1816, and meeting little opposition was pushed through within four days by a vote of 81 to 67. The Senate subsequently passed it even more quickly and by a larger margin than did the House. To prove Johnson's supposition correct, after its adoption Congress adjourned for the year with a finished docket for the first time in its existence.

Yet despite its logic, a recent surge in patriotism, and the economic prosperity of the time, the law proved to be deeply unpopular with many citizens. Thirty years earlier the first Congress had actually proposed as the second constitutional amendment, an article outlawing this very practice. Though the states at the time failed to pass it, concerns over money hungry legislators resonated with many Americans and eventually became the basis for the XXVII Amendment almost 200 years later. Newspapers at the time reported the outrage of citizens towards legislation that was, "poor judgment at best, and treachery at worst ... the names of those members from Maryland who voted for it, are stuck up at all the taverns, stories, blacksmith's shops and cross roads in the country."[147] Johnson himself as author of the legislation was certainly not immune to this outrage and experienced a challenge to his campaign for re-election in 1816. One Kentucky paper opined that, "the opposition to Messrs. Clay and Johnson has every appearance of being very powerful and leads us to expect that they will hereafter be allowed to repent in leisure, of their greediness, in pushing through the compensation bill."[148] In a speech delivered sometime after the affair, Johnson himself noted how the bill, "excited more discontent than the alien or sedition laws, the quasi war with France, the internal taxes of 1798, the embargo, the late war with Great Britain, the treaty of Ghent, or any other measure of the Government from its existence."[149] He goes on to relate how even the most mundane of daily activities, from acquiring a loan to the hiring of help was prefixed with a question on the applicant's view of the Compensation Bill. Johnson's election challenge must have been particularly a shock to him considering his status as a war hero and his unopposed run two years before. His opponent, a Federalist by the name of Benjamin Taylor who was actually a brother-in-law to James Johnson, ran largely on opposition to the new law, estimating that it would cost the nation around $400,000 a year.

Johnson undertook a series of rallies in an attempt to salvage his image, at one point even engaging in a six hour debate with his opponent. Traveling the length and breadth of his district he reminded the voters of his and his family's contributions to both Kentucky and the nation. He often showed them the, "hand (that) was broken in our defense," and detailed his accomplishments in both Congress and in Canada. During one of these speeches he famously compared himself to a trusty Kentucky rifle. If a rifle had fired successfully hundreds of times and only misfired once would you dispose of it? One veteran of the war stood up and challenged the candidate on his support of the law, "do you admit it to be a snap?" Johnson dramatically answered that he did. "Then we will pick the flint and try the old rifle again."[150] The Colonel also enlisted the aid of some of Kentucky's most notable citizens, chief of whom was perhaps the wealthiest man in the state, James Taylor V.[151] In the end Johnson was re-elected by a margin of around 1,000 votes, 600 of which came from Scott County alone where he won by a ratio of five to two. Once back in Congress he joined with the majority of members to repeal his own law, in fact he was the first to rise, declaring that, *"vox populi, vox dei* ... the presumption is, that the people are always right."[152] The pay of Senators and Representatives would remain relatively unchanged until 1855.

In the end though the Republican Party across the nation gained 26 seats in Congress, the facts behind the numbers are startling. Around 68 of the 119 sitting Republican Congressmen were either replaced or else retired in large part due to their participation in the Compensation Law vote, a shocking 57% of their number. When combined with Federalists who also lost re-election, the 14th Congress saw 70% of incumbents lose their sits. In Kentucky in particular, even though the whole state went Republican, only three incumbent Congressmen were returned to office. This small group included Richard Mentor Johnson, Henry Clay, and Joseph Desha. In fact Desha's re-election only came about due to his determined resistance to the law when it first appeared, a position that he consistently reminded the voters of. In this he was the only member of the Congressional delegation from the state who did not vote in favor of the bill. The repeal of the Compensation Bill of 1816 seemed to confirm the Republican theory of vox populi, vox dei. As Johnson himself orated during his speech on the repeal of his own bill, "vigilance is a virtue in a free people."[153]

The effect of this chastisement certainly bore an effect upon Johnson. A decade later while chairman of the Committee of Post Offices and Roads he recommended a $2,000 salary increase for the Postmaster General. Sensitive to the reaction to his previous bill, Johnson made sure to highlight in an almost three page reports the numerous reasons why this raise was warranted. Chief among these reasons was the immense size and complexity of the organization under that position. "All the other branches of the Executive Government, including the Army and Navy, fall short of this number."[154] Likewise Johnson was quick to chastise younger members of Congress in the 1830s when they once again attempted to broach the subject of raising congressional salary.

The various state elections in 1816 would return an even larger Republican majority to Congress. Included among these was once again

Johnson, whose sixth term in the House from 1817 to 1819 would be his last in that chamber for a decade. Both he and his state had eagerly supported the election of James Monroe as President in the Election of 1816. In fact Johnson had once again served as secretary of the Republican presidential election committee. Once the President was in office, Johnson's name was even floated as a potential candidate to be made Secretary of War, but he was passed over for party favorite John C. Calhoun. Instead the senior Representative from Kentucky was picked by his party to serve as the chairman of the Committee on Expenditures for the Department of War, a position he would hold until 1819.

It was while chairman of this committee that Johnson became involved in yet another scandal which threatened to tarnish his political career. In tune with the burgeoning Manifest Destiny ideas of the time, Secretary of War Calhoun set about launching the Yellowstone Expedition in 1819. This journey of discovery, reminiscent of Lewis and Clark's own voyage almost 15 years before, was an immensely popular undertaking at the time. A newspaper editorial described the general zeitgeist as, "the importance of the expedition has attracted the attention of the whole nation, and there is no measure which has been adopted by the present administration that has received such universal commendation."[155] A number of factors colluded to make a show of force by the federal government in the far west desirable and for that purpose Calhoun dispatched a force westward to establish a fort at the convergence of the Yellowstone and Missouri Rivers.

Without much competition or debate Calhoun awarded the contract to fund steamboats and other assorted equipment for the expedition to James Johnson on December 2, 1818. In the finest example of corruption in years, some of the prices listed for items were astronomical while others were simply left blank for James to fill in himself. It is therefore not surprising then that the older Johnson did not provide the most advanced or even functional equipment to the expedition. Out of the five steamboats that were meant to convey the troops westward, two (*Calhoun* and *Exchange*) never even touched water, the *Jefferson* died 30 miles below Franklin, and the aptly named *Johnson* and *Expedition* only managed to reach St. Louis. In fact the economic malfeasance of the elder Johnson helped to ultimately doom the once promising undertaking.

Yet had it not been for a series of contemporaneous events, Johnson's contribution to the failure of the trip would probably have gone unnoticed. In fact the *Kentucky Gazette* congratulated the brothers in October 1819 for their, "Herculean undertaking," and chalked up opposition to simple political posturing.[156] But the onset of the ruinous Panic of 1819 soured many in the country and Congress to the extravagant spending by the War Department. The Johnsons became examples of why a one party system lacking checks and balances is doomed to corruption and failure. Cuts were subsequently made to Calhoun's budget and Congress performed a full investigation. A report by Representative John Alexander Cocke of Tennessee in 1820 revealed that Congress was overcharged by James Johnson for his steamboats by about $76,000.[157] Congress eventually moved to have the whole sum repaid, which helped to financially cripple both Johnsons. As late as the summer of 1820, Richard Mentor Johnson was still seeking contracts for his brother from Calhoun to help pay off their debts, in this case a contract to handle the transportation of supplies to West Point. The Secretary of War recommended that the President make the contract public, no doubt out of both philosophical and political necessity.[158] Yet the incident did not permanently end the career of either Johnson brother, or keep James from serving as an elector for Monroe in 1820.

One of Johnson's last actions as chair of his committee revolved around a seemingly minor event that ended up helping to shape the American political landscape over the next decade. General Andrew Jackson's invasion of Florida in 1818 in pursuit of hostile Indians and subsequent hanging of two British nationals had brought the country close to war with both Spain and the United Kingdom and nearly derailed ongoing negotiations between John Q. Adams and his counterpart in Madrid. Though the White House was eventually able to smooth things over, Jackson's incursion and illegal execution of the two British nationals led to an investigation by Congress. The majority of the committee was against Jackson and penned a scathing report aimed at censuring him, yet Richard Mentor Johnson disagreed and wrote his own minority report. At twice the length of the majority opinion, it exonerated the general and brought Johnson into direct conflict with fellow Kentuckian and anti-Jacksonian, Henry Clay. Johnson's support for Gen. Jackson arose in part due to his own experiences with similar actions along the northwestern border. In the end, despite one of the longest debates in Congressional history, Jackson proved too popular in both the country and in the House for the measure to pass. Johnson himself was the first to take to the floor in support of Jackson, arguing that those who ignored the rules of war, such as these, "pirates on land," deserved death.[159] All of this stood in spite of voting against a measure in June 1812 granting Pres. Madison the ability to seize the same area of East Florida should he see the need to and a subsequent vote in 1819 against the Adams-Onis Treaty that finally acquired the territory.[160] Though he received the eternal thanks of Jackson, threats against his safety in Washington compelled him to carry a firearm about with him for some time afterward.[161]

By 1818 Johnson had decided the time had arrived to move beyond the House and attempt to enter the United States Senate. Under the original Constitution, the state legislature cast votes for Senators, thus making them only indirectly elected by the people. With his family's strong history and connections within the state, the Colonel felt confident of victory. Therefore in December 1818, the Kentucky state legislature gathered, but in the end voted 67-55 in favor of former speaker William Logan to represent their state. It was a crushing blow to the man who prided himself as a home state hero, but his recent scandals as well as political necessities combined to complicate his chances. Despite the loss and resulting offers from the Republican Party to again seek national office, he decided against running once more for his old Congressional seat. A joint resolution was passed by Congress presenting him with a ceremonial sword estimated to have cost $1,200 as thanks for his bravery at the Battle of the Thames and in March 1819 he left the House.[162] As Congressman Philip Pendleton Barbour of Virginia proclaimed in a paean for the hero in March 1818 ...

> "Let it then be remembered that he was zealously in favor of the war. Not content with the distinguished place he held in the councils of the nation, he patriotically resolved to vindicate with his own arm those rights which he had so manfully asserted while voting

for the declaration of war. He erects his standard and proclaims his purpose."[163]

The sword itself was presented in an official ceremony in April 1820 by then President James Monroe. Most of the cabinet officers as well as members of Congress were present as Monroe delivered the following address ...

> "Sir, I now perform an office which is very gratifying to my feelings. In the late war, our country was assailed on every side; on the Atlantic coast and inland frontiers; and in many quarters at the same time. Honored by your fellow citizens, you then held a status in the public council, which afforded a timely opportunity to render services with which a patriotism less ardent would have been satisfied. But you repaired to the field at the head of a regiment of mounted volunteers, and met the enemy at one of the points where he was most formidable. At the head of that corps, and well supporting it, you fought with heroic gallantry, and essentially contributed to the victory which was obtained. Your country is grateful for these services."[164]

Johnson eventually decided to join the Kentucky state legislature rather than simply retire to his farm. No doubt he was hoping to run in the upcoming gubernatorial election the next year. His brother James had attempted to seek the same office in 1816 but to no avail. In the meantime, he worked towards debt relief and the ending of debt imprisonment on the state level, two issues that would eventually garner him more renown upon his return to Washington. Johnson was not to stay too long in Frankfort as the resignation of John J. Crittenden in December opened up the state's other Senate seat. The legislature once again convened, and in a 68-53 vote named Richard Mentor Johnson to be Senator over John Adair, who instead would go on to become governor the next year.

Johnson would spend a decade in the Senate from 1819 to 1829. His arrival in this august body in January 1820 came at one of the pivotal moments in antebellum America. The entrance of Missouri into the nation provoked a firestorm of protest as some northern Congressmen aimed to only admit it as a free state while others sought to combine the admissions of both Maine and Missouri. In January 1820, Sen. Jesse B. Thomas, a Republican from Illinois, proposed that while Missouri should be admitted as a slave state, slavery would thereafter be excluded north of 36°30'. The resolution was referred to a select committee consisting of Thomas [R-Il], James Burrill [F-RI], Richard M .Johnson [R-Ky], William Palmer [R-Vt], and James Pleasants [R-Va]. Several weeks later Johnson stood and gave a lengthy speech against the restriction of slavery by Congress in any part of the nation, preferring to leave it up to the people of the state or territory instead. He astutely pointed out how ...

> "In the District of Columbia, containing a population of 30,000 souls and probably as many slaves as the whole territory of Missouri, the power of providing for their emancipation rests with Congress alone. Why, then, this heart-rending sympathy for the slaves of Missouri, and this cold insensibility, this eternal apathy towards the slaves in the District of Columbia?"[165]

Yet not wishing to see the union broken apart, in February he joined with a slim majority of Senators to unite the Missouri and Maine admission bills together and then helped to push through what became known as the Missouri Compromise against largely Federalist and northern opposition.

True to character, much of his time in the Senate would be spent furthering his efforts to aid those most in need throughout the country. That is not to say that his actions did not also aim to enrich himself as well. In fact he continued to achieve notoriety for his attempts at obtaining government relief for his debts as well as for a series of ethically questionable government sponsored undertakings from which he personally benefited. Likewise Johnson became a lightning rod for patronage, securing jobs for friends and family. One of the clients was his own brother Benjamin who was named a superior judge in Arkansas Territory from 1821 to 1836.

Image 7. Richard Mentor Johnson by Rembrandt Peale

Richard and his brother James were still heavily in debt to the amount of $130,000 due to their part in the Yellowstone Expedition as well as other failed ventures, while his other brother John Telemachus had been ruined by the Panic of 1818. In an effort to settle these debts, Richard attempted to mortgage some of his land holdings in Kentucky to the Second Bank of the United States in June 1820. Though it was normally the policy of the Bank not to become involved in land speculation, fellow Kentuckian and chief counsel for the Bank Henry Clay intervened on his behalf.

> "Col. Richard M Johnson informs me that he has made an application to the Bank of the United States, in behalf of himself and his connections, to be allowed to discharge the debt which they owe that institution in Kentucky, in real estate at valuation ... As a general rule, it must certainly be adverse to the interest of the Bank to invest any portion of its funds in such inactive and unmanageable property as real estate is; but there must be exceptions to it, arising out of the circumstances and conditions of debtors, and I am persuaded that the case of Col. Johnson presents one ... There are

considerations belonging to the case of Col. Johnson, arising out of his public services, his distinguished enterprise, and the esteem in which he is everywhere held, that I am quite sure the Bank will give all the weight to which they ought to receive, in deliberating upon his proposition."[166]

Yet the matter lingered on for some time as the courts and the Bank seemed unsure of how best to handle the issue. Clay writes in a letter to his old War Hawk friend Langdon Cheves in June 1821 that he was, "embarrassed, during the term of the Federal Court, to know what disposition to make of the cases agt. Col. R. M. Johnson & his connexions, as I have not received one line from Philadelphia of direct communication upon that subject."[167] At the same time in an effort to help their financial situation, James began a smelting business on the upper Mississippi but proved unable to correct his losses. As late as 1823 Henry Clay was writing letters on their behalf to Nicholas Biddle of the Bank declaring that, "those gentlemen are utterly unable to discharge their debts; and that any attempt to coerce the payment, by legal means, will be totally unavailing."[168] The debt of the Johnson brothers would not be fully settled with the Bank of the United States until 1824, and leave Richard at this time initially hesitant to dissolve the institution as he himself held at least an estimated 400 shares in it. All of this stands in sharp contrast to the life of younger brother Joel Johnson who after moving to Arkansas in 1831 became one of the wealthiest men in the state, owning 55 slaves and over 2,000 acres in Chicot County, and a member of The Family of politicians who ran the region until the Civil War.[169]

In fact it was largely his own battles with debt that helped to shape his view on debt imprisonment over the next few years. He had achieved some success with the measure back in Kentucky and now hoped to bring it to the national stage. Thus in January 1823, he introduced a measure into the Senate to ban the practice outright. "The principle is deemed too dangerous to be tolerated in a free government, to permit a man for any pecuniary consideration, to dispose of the liberty of his equal."[170] Johnson built his argument around the concept of personal liberty, that, "the power of the creditor to imprison his debtor, is the only case in the United States, where, among free men, one citizen has legal authority to deprive his co-equal fellow citizen ... of the right of personal liberty." His thought is couched heavily in the philosophy of free men unrestrained by oppressive government or class systems. Christianity seemed even to agree with Johnson as he related God's intervention through Elisha in order to aid a widow debtor.[171] "Had poverty been a crime in the sight of God, she would not have been rescued from its consequences by a miracle." Likewise as no man has been perfected by God and the power of even the government is limited, the granting of the power to imprison others to citizens is both extreme and illogical. For a man whose family sought eagerly after wealth and power, Johnson argued for virtue, honor, and benevolence to be used as the measure of a man. "Riches are the idol of the world, and ever have been," a quick look at the fates of Judas Iscariot and Benedict Arnold, according to Johnson, was all that was necessary to prove this truism. Finally, as the true debtor lacks the means by which to pay his debt, jailing them in the hopes of acquiring some, "hidden treasure," is likewise nonsensical.

Some of the strongest opposition to his plan though came not from creditors but from strict constructionists. These legislators doubted the state's power to eliminate the practice as the Constitution clearly vested the ability to establish bankruptcy laws in Congress, Johnson was quick to point to the precedent set by the recent case of Sturges v Crowninshield. This case, which was argued before the Supreme Court in February 1819, dealt with New York's ability to pass bankruptcy law. The Marshall Court went on to rule unanimously in the state's favor thus providing to Johnson fodder for his belief that states could not only pass bankruptcy law but modify preexisting ones to eliminate debtors prison as a recourse for creditors.

Yet despite his best efforts and loft oratory, few were moved to action. Even the states themselves were slow to respond, with Kentucky being one of the first and few to act. Undeterred, Johnson continued to submit the bill to Congress almost every year until the end of his time in the Senate. It passed the upper house twice but for a variety of reasons repeatedly failed in the lower house. Even former President Madison took the opportunity to write Johnson about the issue in April 1824 stating that, "your Speech & that of my neighbour in the same House, on the same subject have infused great force into the appeal to the public sensibility. The views taken of the subject are well calculated to promote a meliorating revision of the law; and your success has my hearty wishes."[172] His committee's report was finally accepted in January 1832 and the government then moved to ban the practice at the federal level soon after. Johnson's continued efforts on behalf of the people of his state in both this and other measures led to his unanimous re-election to the Senate for a six-year term in 1822. At the same time, his brother James was elected to the House of Representatives serving from 1825 until his death in 1826.

Once re-elected, Johnson became involved with perhaps one of the most bizarre proposals in the Senate's history. Captain John Cleves Symmes of Ohio had been traveling the nation on a series of speaking tours in which he proposed an expedition to the north or south pole. Failing to gain the attention, or money, of any notable citizens, he next turned to Richard Mentor Johnson. While a petition brought by a Congressman for the purpose of exploration was not a novelty, the reasoning behind Symmes' expedition was unique. This "scientist" was a believer in the Hollow Earth Theory, which held that the planet was a hollow shell. If one penetrated the roughly 600–800-mile-thick crust either through digging or by accessing the openings that were presumed to lie at the north and south pole, an expedition could explore the interior of the planet. Inside were to be found plants, animals, minerals, rivers, seas, and untold riches. As ludicrous as the idea sounds, Johnson was not the only one to be interested in funding an attempt. Several prominent members of President John Q. Adams' cabinet offered their support, though his short time in office prevented any serious consideration. In March 1822, Senator Johnson dutifully submitted to Congress a petition to advance Symmes' voyage of discovery complete with funding for two ships of around 300 tons and assorted equipment. Initially there was some debate between Senators Johnson and Archer as to whether it should be referred to the committees on foreign relations or commerce since it involved both diplomacy and trade. Several months later on January 27, 1823, his brother John Telemachus Johnson submitted a similar petition to the House. It is curious as to whether the brothers once again hoped for lucrative contracts to equip the expedition. Though the idea was brought up again the next year by Sen. Ruggles of Ohio and even eventually received 46 votes in Congress, it ultimately failed to pass.[173]

Less bizarrely, Johnson proposed his own amendment to the Constitution during the winter of 1821–1822. In a speech before Congress on January 14, 1822, he reminded his fellow legislators that the amendment process was one of the great innovations of the Founding Fathers. It was a tool gleaned from the ancient republics of the Mediterranean that had allowed those states to adapt and evolve for hundreds of years. He then proceeds to address the nature of his concern with the current constitutional system, namely the, "conflicts between the federal judiciary and the sovereignty of the states."[174] An amendment was necessary to prevent the, "Egyptian darkness," which was slowly beginning to cloud the legal landscape of the nation after 40 years. Numerous cases had arisen during this time which slowly stripped more power away from the states. Some of the more notable examples were McCulloch v Maryland, Gibbons v Ogden, and Dartmouth v Woodward. Johnson's amendment would have given the Senate appellate jurisdiction in all future suits between the federal government and states.

His concern in this was purely philosophical, for as a staunch Republican he was opposed to the encroaching federal authority which to him symbolized the last gasp of the Federalist Party. His amendment would serve to partially reverse the pattern in place since Marbury v Madison and stood in a similar light to the Kentucky and Virginia Resolutions of Jefferson and Madison. Johnson's view would rest well with today's opponents of judicial activism. In a democratic society built upon the concept of federalism, why were a handful of unelected judges able to overrule the will of the people? Though in the end it obviously failed to garner the necessary votes it once again exposes the Jeffersonian philosophy of the man.

The contentious Election of 1824 brought an end to the Era of Good Feelings and found a new shining star for Johnson to follow. Though Secretary of the Treasury William Crawford was considered the heir presumptive to Monroe, a serious stroke cast doubt upon his health and threw the election wide open. A series of favorite son candidates, including Andrew Jackson from the south, John Q. Adams from the north, and Henry Clay from the west, emerged to fill the void. In the end while Jackson pulled the most votes, no candidate had the necessary majority needed to win. The Constitution was prepared for such an event and the top three vote getters had their names thrown into Congress for a second vote.

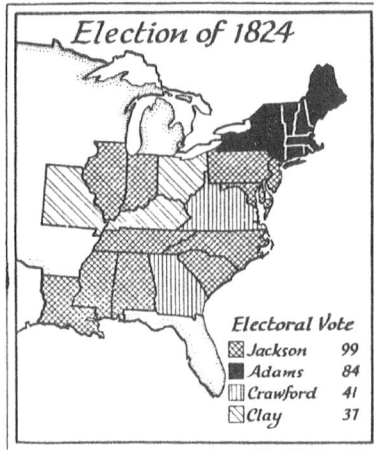

Image 8. The Election of 1824

Richard Mentor Johnson had initially supported his fellow Kentuckian, Henry Clay, as did his state's electors. This backing undoubtedly arose from a number of factors, including their mutual home state, their War Hawk heritage, common beliefs in internal improvements to aid the west, and Clay's handling of Johnson's debt issues. As early as 1822, Johnson wrote to Clay reassuring the latter that he was, "incapable of promoting anything unfavorable to you," and should Clay need it, "I could be of service to you."[175] Yet as Clay garnered the least votes initially his name was not one of the three advanced to Congress for consideration. Thus, Johnson was free to vote for whomever he wished to. In terms of his views on both political and economic issues, Johnson was more in line with the thinking of Andrew Jackson than John Q. Adams and began to vigorously support the former in the contingency election. Rumors even began to float at the time that Jackson was seriously considering Johnson as his choice for Secretary of War.

Quite ironically it was the occasionally corrupt Kentuckian who broke the news to Jackson of the infamous Corrupt Bargain that had taken place between his fellow Kentucky Senator, Clay, and Adams. In exchange for being named Secretary of State, Henry Clay convinced the Representatives from Kentucky and several other states to throw their support behind Adams. Undoubtedly many in the state felt that having a Kentuckian in the cabinet and positioned as the heir-apparent would better serve their state, though Johnson at the term referred to the representative's choice of Adams as, "an uphill business in Kentucky."[176] The fury of Jackson and his supporters led to the reemergence of a two party system in the country with the rise of the National Republicans and the Democratic Party. Johnson, now a loyal Jackson man, quickly emerged as a leading western Democrat. In fact it was he who announced the fury that was to follow for the next four years as Jackson's party sought to destroy Adams'. "The administration will be put down, though it were as pure as the angels in heaven."[177]

His next four years in the Senate were passed in relative calm. A functional paralysis between the supporters and opponents of Jackson descended upon Congress. When combined with the continuing economic prosperity and peace at home and abroad, matters discussed and legislation passed tended to be mundane. Johnson continued to submit petitions on the behalf of various individuals and carried on his annual campaign against debt imprisonment. The only pieces of legislation of note to be introduced were a variety of Indian treaties and the dispatch of an American legation to a Pan-American conference in Central America.

The dawning of the 1828 election cycle brought fear to Johnson who was concerned that, "the admn party will unite upon some Jackson man & oust him from the Senate- So that he will be upon his good behavior."[178] As Kentucky Congressman John Chambers wrote at the time, Johnson had, "gone over," to the Jackson party.[179] Yet despite his loyal support for the party, it proved to be less than supportive of him. The Democratic Party grew to feel that for a variety of reasons Johnson had become a liability to Jackson's own chances of election in 1828 and quietly moved to ruin his re-election to the Senate that year. His own brother, John Telemachus Johnson, a member of the Kentucky legislature, was forced to withdraw his name from consideration for the seat, a move readily approved of by Clay's allies in Kentucky.[180] Upon hearing the news Johnson declared, "I have uniformly looked to the people for office; I have never expressed a wish that I desired any office in the gift of the government; and I have preferred serving in my present situation to any other, because of my gratitude to those who first honored me, and have continued their confidence when placed before them. In the twenty-four years that I have served in the legislature and in Congress, I have never been more than the same number of days absent from my duty."[181] Proud of his record and undisturbed by this political rebuke, Johnson returned to his home state and was once again elected to the House of Representatives, defeating incumbent Robert McHatton who had been chosen to fill his brother James Johnson's seat upon the latter's death in 1826. For the next eight years, Richard Mentor Johnson continued his fight on behalf of the common man in true Jacksonian fashion.

One of his most famous achievements during this time was his Sunday Mail Report. So well respected was this speech by Johnson that people allegedly had it printed on satin and hung it in their parlors as words of wisdom.[182] Praise continued to flow in for years afterward with the citizens of Baton Rouge presenting him with a silver goblet in 1833. In actuality much of the report was probably ghostwritten by Obadiah Brown, the chief clerk in the Washington post office whom Johnson occasionally roomed with, or the famed evangelist Alexander Campbell as Johnson himself, "possessed neither the education nor ability to write such a document."[183]

A bill was presented to Congress in 1829 to halt the delivery of mail on Sundays, largely on religious grounds. The nation was in the middle of the Second Great Awakening and a Protestant fury was sweeping the land. Johnson's opposition to the bill came from more than just the fact that he was a partisan supporter of the concept of the separation of church and state. A certain element of anti-religiosity was emerging in the country. Though this is often common during times of religious revival as a natural counter-reaction, this movement was more catalyzed by the common man democratic values of Jackson supporters. Organized religion represented for some the politics of elitism and separation that were plaguing them financially and politically. Johnson associated the intrusion of religion into politics with the Congregationalists and behind them his old adversary the Federalists. As Chairman of the Committee on Post Offices and Post Roads, Johnson delivered the final report on the bill. His speech became a legendary defense of the concept of the wall of separation and has been quoted from ever since.

"That some respite is required from the ordinary vocations of life, is an established principle, sanctioned by the usages of all nations, whether Christian or Pagan ... If kept within its legitimate sphere of action, no injury can result from its observance. It should, however, be kept in mind, that the proper object of government is to protect all persons in the enjoyment of their religious as well as civil rights, and not to determine for any whether they shall esteem one day above another, or esteem all days alike holy ... the committee would hope that no portion of the citizens of our country would willingly introduce a system of religious coercion in our civil institutions ... It is not the legitimate province of the legislature to determine what religion is true or what false ... If the observance or a holy day become incorporated in our institutions, shall we not forbid the movement of an army, prohibit an assault in time of war, and lay an injunction upon our naval officers to lie in the wind while upon the ocean on that day? ... Let the professors of Christianity recommend their religion by deeds of benevolence—by Christian meekness—by love of temperance and holiness. Let them combine their efforts to instruct the ignorant, to relieve the widow and the orphan, to promulgate to the world the gospel of their Saviour, recommending its precepts by their habitual example; government will find its legitimate object in protecting them. It cannot oppose them, and they will not need its aid. Their moral influence will then do infinitely more to advance the true interests of religion than any measures they may call on Congress to enact."[184]

Perhaps most telling was the fact that the Senate accepted his resolution with very little dissension. As mentioned, a strong anti-religious sentiment was taking hold in parts of the nation and in the Democratic Party in particular. Johnson himself estimated that for every one person who favored abandoning Sunday delivery, four more opposed it.[185]

The popularity of the resolution helped to solidify Johnson in the eyes of many liberals as a defender of individual liberties against the encroachment of state religion. At the 95th anniversary celebration of Thomas Paine's birthday which was hosted by Tammany Hall in 1832 Johnson and his Sunday Mail Report was the subject of the most toasts after Paine himself. In fact the first toast of the night, which was delivered by the President of the Tammany Society, was to, "Col. Richard M. Johnson—The bold and fearless advocate and defender of civil and religious liberty. His Sunday Mail Reports entitle him to the gratitude of every Republican and lover of practical liberal principles."[186] While still a further member stated that Johnson's report, "has been correctly designated a clear exposition of, or commentary on, the 'Declaration of Rights,' in as far as regards the rights of conscience."[187] Nor was this the only occurrence over the next few years of the amount of praise that was showered upon the Senator. The lasting popularity of his words are attested to by the fact that excerpts from his speech are still used by organizations and persons in favor of the separation of church and state even today.

This move was even more striking when one considers that one of Richard's brothers was the famed evangelist John Telemachus Johnson. Educated at Transylvania University, John had passed the bar and operated a successful mill, eventually acquiring 500 acres of land before being ruined by the Panic of 1818. He subsequently served in both the House of Representatives as well as the Kentucky legislature. John was a lifelong Baptist, like most of his family. In fact in 1810 James Johnson had built a brick Baptist church at Great Crossing, the first such structure in all of Scott County. Yet John ultimately had an awakening in 1831, thanks to the efforts of Thomas and Alexander Campbell and joined the Disciples of Christ. "My eyes were opened and a new interest awakened in Christianity. I felt I owed to that man of God, A. Campbell, a debt of gratitude no language can express."[188] He soon abandoned his promising political career and became a well-respected preacher. His life ultimately revolved around the church, publishing various periodicals associated with it and gaining thousands of converts. Finally, he was responsible for the founding of Bacon College which eventually became Kentucky University.

During his time in the House, Johnson also remained a staunch supporter of the movement west of people. Like many western politicians, he was a true believer in the freedom and opportunity offered by the American frontier. As early as 1822, as part of the Senate Committee on Roads and Canals, Johnson had helped to earmark funds for the repair of the Cumberland Road, a move heartily endorsed by Henry Clay who had written Johnson asking whether, "it is going to decay with a much greater rapidity than it was erected."[189] Yet panics, unorganized land purchases, corruption, and basic ignorance had resulted in hundreds of thousands of Americans living in the territories west of the Mississippi being in danger of losing the land which they had only recently acquired. Congressman Johnson worked hard to secure the passage of a number of bills aimed at improving their situation. One allowed for the half million or so farmers in danger of foreclosure to keep the portions of land that they had paid off, losing only those pieces which they had not. Another bill called for allowing persons who had moved west and improved upon their land to purchase it at cost. Both measures proved to be immensely popular with western debtors and did much to spur the continued development of the frontier.

It was in this same vein, and with a bit of provincial interest, that Johnson supported the Maysville Road Bill in 1830. Designed as a section of the National Road, the highway was to be constructed from Lexington to Maysville, Ky. Due to its geographic confinement, Jackson and most other Democrats refused to support the bill. Johnson personally lobbied the President on the bill's behalf, stating that there was no road, "more traveled, and none of the same extent by which you can promote the common good," but to no avail.[190] After it passed, through a combination of Whig action and support from western lawmakers, Jackson vetoed the measure on May 27, 1830. Johnson's unwillingness to overturn the President's veto damaged his image in Kentucky and helped lead to his defeat to Henry Clay in the Senatorial election the next year.

When Jackson began his war against the Second Bank of the United States, Richard Mentor Johnson once again served as a loyal supporter. His previous experiences with the First Bank meant that he needed little goading to back Jackson's views. In a letter to the head of the Bank Nicholas Biddle, Leslie Combs including Johnson's name as one of the chief opponents to the institution. "Gen. J says the Bk in unconstitutional. Mr. Van Buren echoes the opinion and old Tecumseh follows suit."[191] In the end, he voted against re-chartering of the institution and famously said that the Bank, like all corporations, "controlled by persons, irresponsible to the people, are liable to exercise a dangerous influence, and corporate bodies generally, especially when they have the power to effect the circulating medium of the country, do not well comport with genius of a republic," similar to sentiments expressed years later with regards to the Federal Reserve and the growth of the crony capitalism.[192]

Johnson was also chairman of the Committee of Military Affairs during the 1830s. His personal experience with warfare, especially confronting the Indians out west, would serve him and the country well in this position. One of his most notable, selfless, and at the same time personally damning acts in this role was his committee's investigation of claims against Gen. William Henry Harrison in 1831. Ever since his victories at Tippecanoe and the Thames, a variety of charges had arisen against the great commander often disparagingly referred to as "Granny Harrison." Johnson personally helped to not only clear Harrison of any possibility of censure or rebuke but also delivered a proud address praising his former commander, a speech would later be used against him by every newspaper in the nation during the presidential elections of 1836 and 1840. "Of the career of General Harrison I need not speak- the history of the West, is his history. For forty years he has been identified with its interests, its perils, and its hopes ... During the late war, he was longer in active service than any other General Officer; he was perhaps oftener in action than any of them, and NEVER SUFFERED A DEFEAT."[193]

Besides his usual efforts to obtain pensions and land for veterans and their families, the Senator also crafted a series of bills to improve the capabilities of the military. One of these, HR 646, was proposed in

December 1832 and aimed to strengthen the ability of the army to respond to Native attacks and raids. Entitled "A Bill for the More Perfect Defense of the Frontier," it sought to replace a newly established corps of rangers with one of mounted dragoons. Likewise on April 19, 1834, Johnson oversaw the passage of a bill that mandated the printing of 5,000 copies of a manual on cavalry tactics. His own experience with this branch of service back in 1812 helped to convince him of the need to maintain a strong cavalry corps in the U.S. Army. His efforts would in fact pay dividends a decade later during the Mexican War. Finally, in May 1836 he spoke out in favor of repaying the southern states for their expenditures during the most recent Seminole War in Florida.

> "When this murderous, savage war broke out in Florida, which has spread ruin and desolation to many families, and half depopulated some fair portions of that flourishing Territory, the hostile trump was heard from Charleston to New Orleans; and the patriotic citizens of South Carolina, Georgia, Alabama, and Louisiana, not willing to wait the dull delays of this House for authority, while their fellow-citizens were bleeding under the scalping knife of the savages, flew to arms ... The service was national ... They justly regarded the citizens of that territory as a branch of the American family."[194]

These various issues combined to convince Johnson of the need for a volunteer-based military. Building upon his own experiences in both Kentucky against the Northwest Indians and with his own volunteer unit in Canada, Johnson argued for the adoption of volunteer units to engage the growing Indian threat in the west. He provided the Senate with a letter from then Secretary of War Lewis Cass which called for, "in the event of any difficulties among the Indians, I consider the measure undertaken by the Military Committee, of allowing volunteer corps to be taken into service for a term not exceeding twelve months."[195] Existing law allowed the President to call out the militia for three months. Yet the geographic and temporal natures of Indian warfare were expansive and did not suit short-term military action. The new law would allow the President to accept volunteer militia units for longer periods of time. While some were concerned with the constitutional effect of this or otherwise feared the immense amount of power it could potentially give to the President, Johnson provided a distinct litany of reasons why the new law would better serve the nation. He argued that the current system was detrimental towards the poor and farmers as it represented an outdated system of corvée labor. Volunteers would tend to be, "young men, who are animated by the ardor of youth, impelled by the thirst of glory, urged by the fire of patriotism, and willing to learn the duties of the camp and the field, while indulging the novelties so grateful to youthful minds."[196] Likewise disease, always the perennial enemy of a campaign, would be more likely to hit the weak, elderly, and infirm who are forcibly drafted into service, while young volunteers would be more resilient. Overall Johnson was recommending the type of volunteer army that became popular again in the post-Vietnam era, and army of willing, young specialists dedicated to the completion of a campaign. Johnson urged immediate action on this bill as, "the cloud which is gathering in our western horizon warns us to make immediate preparation for the approaching storm."[197]

In a similar vein, that same year Johnson spoke out in Congress in favor of providing relief to the city of New York. On the evening of December 16, 1835, a massive conflagration erupted in lower Manhattan. Over a dozen city blocks were eventually reduced to rubble and ash before the fire was finally extinguished. Losses were in the millions of dollars with numerous insurance companies among the casualties. Because of this, Johnson recommended that the U.S. Congress help to fund the rebuilding of the greatest port in the nation. Precedence alone along with Christian charity demanded it. "The United States has been liberal, generous to the victims of Carracas, and by his vote should not be less liberal to our citizens of New York, who had suffered by the late dreadful conflagration."[198]

Richard Mentor Johnson's time in Congress was a combination of notable accomplishments and base scandals. He became well known in many parts of the country for his efforts on behalf of debtors, his opposition to debt imprisonment, his army reform measures, and the bills he helped pass for widows and veterans. Yet at the same time his scandalous appropriations of money for him and his family, his proposal to tunnel to the center of the planet, and unpopular pieces of legislation also assured him a certain level of notoriety. Johnson himself summed up the accomplishments of his time in Congress in the following way ...

> "I will hazard to the assertion that no Congress, since the peace of 1783, has greater claims upon the confidence of the people; and by their acts they will be judged. Has the volunteer lost his only horse, this Congress has made provision to pay him; has the faithful soldier arrearages of pay due him, the last session made ample appropriations; does the wounded, bleeding invalid present himself as indigent and unable to procure his living by his labor, he is placed upon the pension list; has the widow lost her husband at the plains of the Raisin or elsewhere, while in the service of the United States, the balm of consolation is administered to the bleeding heart in the five years' half pay."[199]

Truly this was a Congress and a Congressman of the people.

CHAPTER V

ROMANCE AND THE ROCKY ROAD TO THE VICE PRESIDENCY

The issue that continued to damage Johnson's image on the national stage concerned his personal relationship back in Kentucky. The story of his marriage has been viewed as foolish, an abomination, unwise, romantic, or abusive depending upon the generation and the viewpoint of the commentator. Yet one thing is for certain, at the time it became a major hindrance to his political fortunes, dooming a variety of opportunities including his Senate career.

According to a variety of biographies, Richard Mentor Johnson was early on involved in a romance that his mother disapproved of, most likely because of the woman's social standing. Very little additional information is provided but it apparently soured him against marriage for the rest of his life or at least sent him down a bitter path of nonconformity and revenge. With the family's desire for power and wish for advancement in Kentucky society, this fact stands out as highly peculiar. As previously discussed, his sisters all married the prominent military men, while many of his brothers married the daughters of other men of ability. Perhaps the best example would be John Telemachus Johnson who wedded Sophia Lewis, the daughter of a federal judge, in 1811. Yet despite his lack of a marriage that is not to say that his life did not have love. In fact one Whig newspaper later claimed rather tongue in cheek that, "Col. Johnson is entitled to as much credit for this astonishing increase of population in the Western States, as Gen. Jackson."[200]

Besides being a military hero and a successful politician, Johnson was also a rather prosperous slave owner at certain points. From owning 12 slaves in 1810 he expanded his plantation to over 74 by 1820. Yet for a variety of reasons he reduced the number of slaves on his property to 45 in 1830 and by the time of his death in 1850 there are only seven slaves listed on census returns. Many of his initial slaves undoubtedly came from his father who has already been described as a successful farmer in the region. He remained a staunch defender of the practice throughout his life, once describing the attempt by Congress to ban slavery in Missouri as, "the heart sickens, the tongue falters."[201] During the same debate he foreshadowed the very circumstances that would eventually split the nation in two. "Still more cautious should we be about intermeddling with the right of property and self-government in Missouri. In so doing, you will jeopardize the harmony of the Union, which may possibly ultimate in a civil war."[202] Yet his view was hardly that of an unrepentant fire-eater. Johnson held much to the same view of slavery as Calhoun, as a benefit to both parties, if it is carried out properly, and an institution that the spreading of which would actually help to eventually drive to extinction.[203]

Sometime around the death of his father in 1815, Johnson acquired a slave woman by the name of Julia Ann Chinn. While some sources suggest that she was an inheritance from his father's estate her exact origins remain a mystery. There were a number of Chinn families in Kentucky during the time period and yet none are recorded in Virginia in the 1790 Census. This would lean towards the assumption that she was possibly purchased by Robert after he had relocated the family to Kentucky. Interestingly, there is a Col. William Chinn who was living at Bryan's Station while the Johnsons were there, having moved west himself from Virginia and marrying Sarah Bryan at the fort in 1792. He is recorded as being a slave owner, possessing several in the 1810 Census and living only a few miles away from the Johnsons at George-town. Though William Chinn died in 1814, his widow (two of who's sons were killed or captured at the River Raisin Massacre) continued to reside in the area, but interestingly enough is recorded as having no slaves in 1820. It is possible that Robert or Richard purchased Julia Ann Chinn sometime during this decade; geography, circumstantial evidence, their own pecuniary interest, and the rarity of the surname certainly allow for it. William Chinn's age also allows for him to pos-sibly have been the father of Julia as she was born around the time of his marriage.

As for herself, Julia was claimed by Johnson's supporters at the time to be an octaroon, a slave who was only ⅛ black. Yet even with only one of her great-grandparents being black she could still legally be a slave and Johnson was not at liberty to marry her. However with the near absence of birth records and affirmed paternities for slaves, the above fact is simply conjecture. His opponents more often than not described Julia as a mulatto, a general catchall for a mixed slave, as a way to denigrate the relationship still further. Either way the romance was certainly scandalous, and we can imagine his mother certainly regretting her condemnation of his earlier affair. The two maintained a common-law marriage for years with Julia even serving as hostess to Pres. James Monroe and Gen. Andrew Jackson during their tour of the state in July 1819 as well as to the Marquis de Lafayette during his visit to the plantation in May 1824. She was a competent manager of his plantation, a devoted wife and mother, and a God fearing woman, being a member of Great Crossings Baptist Church. She made sure their children received the best education available in the state with their daughters famously entertaining the French general with their piano playing during his visit.[204]

The Congressman's actions were not only scandalous to many at the time but also widely discussed in newspapers due to his public position. George Prentice of the *Louisville Journal* wrote that, "if Col. Johnson had the decency and decorum to seek to hide his ignominy from the world, we would refrain from lifting the curtain."[205] Another partisan writer in Kentucky, Duff Green, once described Julia in quite unflattering terms as, "a jet-black, thick-lipped, odiferous negro wench." A historian only a few years after the death of Johnson referred to the former Vice President as, "that Ethiop-loving demagogue."[206] During the campaign of 1836 a Whig newspaper, while praising the affection of the man regretted that they were wasted on this, "sausage-liped Julia," rather than, "a proper object."[207] Yet the crime committed by Johnson was not his physical relationship with his slave as this was quite common at the time, nor was it the fact that he had two children with Julia, the real crime according to Green and others was that he "reared a family of children whom he endeavored to force upon society as equals."

Richard Johnson would have two daughters with Julia, Imogene Chinn Johnson and Adaline Chinn Johnson.[208] The birthdates of both girls around 1812 would seem to imply that either Johnson and Chinn were already romantically involved *before* she officially became his property with the death of Robert Johnson in 1815 or else that he received her as property before that point. Their mother handled most of the upbringing and education of the girls and worked towards marrying both off to white men. Their tutor, Thomas Henderson, expressed his shock at the ability of the girls to fully pass for white and at their keen intellect and, "uncommon aptitude ... to take learning."[209] By these actions Julia achieved the goals of her family for four generations by assuring that they and their children were now considered legally white.[210] Yet not everyone in Kentucky looked favorably on the Johnson family marriages. A Whig periodical reported on the marriage of Adaline that, "this is the second time that the moral feelings of that part of the people of Scott County, who possess such feelings, have been shocked and outraged by the marriage of a mulatto daughter of Col. Johnson to a white man, if a man who will so far degrade himself; who will make himself an object of scorn and destation to every person ... for a little property can be considered a white man."[211] Foreseeing the actions of the courts after his death, Johnson himself presented Thomas Scott and his new wife with a portion of Blue Spring Farm.

Johnson never apologized for his relationships, famously stating that, "unlike Jefferson, Clay, Poindexter and others, I married my wife under the eyes of God, and apparently He has found no objections." George Prentice answered Johnson's comparison to Jefferson by stating that, "he (Jefferson) never lived in open intercourse with an 'odiferous wench'; he never bribed 'his fellow white citizens' to 'make such beasts of themselves' before the open eyes of the whole world as to stand up in church, grasp the sable paws of negresses and pronounce the sacred vows of wedlock."[212] Though Kentucky, much like practically every other state in the union, had a miscegenation law on the books forbidding marriage between a white and a mulatto, Julia Chinn as an octaroon would have been exempted from this code as would have been her daughters.[213] In a nod to Johnson's conduct though, the new constitution of Kentucky which passed in 1850, the year of his death, required any manumitted slaves be expelled from the state. The shunning of his family was said to be commonplace. In one famous anecdote, the war hero Johnson was delivering a 4th of July oration in 1828 but his daughters were jostled out of the pavilion where they were seated due to their race. Johnson angrily finished up his address, threw his children into a carriage, and drove off.

Image 9. Imogene Johnson and Her Husband

Yet not all were dismayed by the prospect or sight of Johnson's wife. Socialite Margaret Bayard Smith, the wife of Samuel Harrison Smith who was a famed newspaper editor and President of the Washington branch of the Bank of the United States, recorded many pleasurable encounters with Julia Chinn in the 1820s. In a letter to a friend written in 1827, Smith described Johnson's wife as a, "little woman [who] improves exceedingly on acquaintance. I tell her she is too good for a mere fashionable lady ... she has great simplicity of manners and her living and dressing in the highest style and the consequent flattery and attention she receives has not in the least spoil'd a natural kind and sensible disposition."[214] Smith also records seeing Julia Johnson at a party hosted by James Fenimore Cooper in 1824, clearly some in Washington society not only tolerated but encouraged her presence.[215]

Julia Chinn would not live to see Richard's greatest achievement, dying of cholera in 1833 during the Second Cholera Epidemic which was sweeping the globe. Yet as one later periodical reported, "his unnatural appetites had rendered negro love necessary to him."[216] After the death of his common law wife, Johnson allegedly began a relationship with another slave, possibly a niece of Julia, named Patience Chinn, daughter of Johnson's brother-in-law Daniel Chinn. Other sources at the time named her instead as Parthene. Not much is known about this woman except for stories and rumors that after she cheated on him, the

Senator had her sold off. A letter to the Louisville Journal related the event as, "Johnson's second wife, Madame Parthene, a yellow woman, has eloped with one of his Indian students, carrying with her a check for $1,000 and cash to the amount of $300, which she took from her titled husband's drawer, she having possession of his keys. The name of the Indian is Jones, and he is a fine looking copper-faced savage. One of Johnson's first wive's nieces and Mrs. Johnson were out on horseback and met Jones."[217] Instead the Congressman began to be romantically involved with her sister Lucy. One contemporary commenter described the latter woman to Pres. Van Buren as, "a young Delilah of about the complexion of Shakespears swarthy Othello."[218] In 1848, the renowned black abolitionist Henry Highland Garnet described her as a, "Cleopatra."[219] Daniel Chinn himself alleged that Johnson had all of the women and all of his children with them sold into slavery to a James Peak.[220] Census records show Johnson living with a Patience Chinn in 1850 (the year of his death), so it is highly unlikely that he ever sold this woman off.[221]

A slave named Lucy (Chinn?) did live at the nearby Mitchell Plantation in Mason County. She married Henry Alexander in 1832, but already had a daughter by an unknown husband in 1826. Some historians claim that Johnson was the father of this child named Maria Alexander whose own daughter, Harriet Aletha Gibbs Marshall (1865–1941), went on to become a leader in field of black music around the turn of the twentieth century.[222] Johnson's almost fanatical fetish with the women of the Chinn family merely served to magnify the disgust of contemporary observers.

Due to these affairs and rumored liaisons, his political career became seriously tarnished. It was quite telling that the Senate doorkeeper once referred to him as, "the most vulgar man of all the vulgar men of this world."[223] Even after his death, Johnson's mixing of the races was used as political fodder by Abraham Lincoln during his famed debate with Stephen Douglas for a Senate seat. Attempting to downplay his own antislavery views, the future President pointed out that he had no intention of seeking equality between the races or even intermarriage, only a certain Democratic Vice President had done that.

> "I will add to this that I have never seen to my knowledge a man, woman or child who was in favor of producing a perfect equality—social and political—between negroes and white men. I recollect but one distinguished instance that I ever heard of so frequently as to be entirely satisfied of its correctness—and that is the case of Judge Douglas' old friend Col. Richard M. Johnson."[224]

Yet using Johnson's alleged amalgamation as campaign fodder was more of a political tincture. After all numerous other Democrats including Thomas Jefferson had had similar relationships, with some, including James Henry Hammond, going even farther into the field of perversion. Johnson's real crime was his political views. As mentioned earlier, the Republican Party was evolving from the party of landed, aristocratic, southern farmers into the modern Democratic party of egalitarianism for the masses. Johnson's view on debt relief, internal improvements, and his political style clashed sharply with the more conservative Democrats of Virginia.[225] Yet it was easier to rally the masses against him by his personal actions than his political stances, thus the Democrats often ran more against Julia Chinn than Richard Mentor Johnson.

Colonel Johnson's road to the office of Vice President began just before President Jackson's second election. Due to the Nullification Crisis, the Petticoat Affair, and a variety of personality conflicts, Jackson and his closest associates in the Democratic Party were intent on dumping Vice President John C. Calhoun. Johnson worked hard to patch up differences between the two men, giving credence to one historian who referred to him as having, "the rare quality of being personally liked by everyone," but to no avail.[226] He had played a similar role three years before when the President had used him as a mediator with the cabinet during the Petticoat Affair. Jackson returned the favor by naming Benjamin Johnson to be the first federal district judge in Arkansas in 1836. Johnson was clearly an interesting choice for this mission as many at the time compared his own lack of morality and the forcing of his amalgamated relationship to the situation of Peggy Eaton.[227]

Though the party quickly re-nominated Jackson for the presidency they were split as to who should be his running mate and called a national convention. Ely Moore, the leader of the Working Men's Party in New York, supported Johnson for the position of Vice President due to his opposition to religious interference in government and his support of debtors. Yet larger factors were at play in the nominating process. In a way reminiscent of Franklin Roosevelt's fourth election in 1944, insiders expressed concern about the health of the President. Jackson would be 66 years old at his next inauguration, making him the oldest man yet to take the chief executive's chair. Though John Adams would have been roughly the same age if he had been re-elected, the latter was in much better health and in fact lived for another 26 years after his defeat in 1800. John McLean, a justice on the Supreme Court, opined to John Norvell that Jackson was in "feeble health" and could die during his second term. As such, McLean questioned whether Johnson possessed the necessary abilities to succeed the President should his death occur.[228] While Jackson would complete his second term and even ponder a third, he ultimately died only nine years after stepping down. Though Johnson had no serious prospects of winning the nomination, he continued to actively push for the position until Jackson's campaign manager, William Berkeley Lewis, personally convinced him to abandon his efforts. In May 1832 at the Athenaeum in Baltimore, where the Democratic National Convention had gathered, the vote was over quickly. Martin Van Buren of New York, who clearly had a geographical advantage that Jackson needed, received 208 votes. Richard Johnson finished a distant third behind the favorite of southerners, Philip Pendleton Barbour, polling only 26 delegates from Kentucky, Illinois, and Indiana.

Knowing that Jackson would most likely not run for a third term in 1836, Johnson and his supporters began to campaign for the party's nomination only shortly after the 1832 election had been finalized. Ely Moore remained a staunch supporter of the Congressman claiming him to be, "the friend of pure religion, by guarding it against a contaminating alliance with politics."[229] The western states in particular began to flock to the banner of their favorite son. Duff Green's paper told at the time how, "the western states are flooded with handbills nominating Col. Richard M. Johnson, of Kentucky, as candidate for the Presidency in 1836."[230] Foreshadowing modern campaigns, Johnson's supporters enlisted the aid of various artists, entertainers, writers, and media outlets to begin pushing his candidacy early. In 1833, William Emmons of Boston published *The Authentic Biography of Col. Richard Mentor Johnson.* This idyllic version of the life of the Congressman served as a propaganda piece to introduce Johnson to those outside of Kentucky. In New York, Richard Emmons wrote a play about Johnson's great victory entitled, "Tecumseh, or, the Battle of the Thames," performances of which allegedly included the authentic pistol with which he shot the chief.[231] Theater-goers witnessed the gallantry of Johnson as the villains of the War of 1812, including Tecumseh and Gen. Chambers, discussed his prowess as a warrior. "He must a warrior be- but in the Senate."[232] For his own part the heroic Johnson, who doesn't appear on stage until the fourth act, delighted audiences with both his oratorical brilliance and frequent praises of Jackson. A poem written by the same playwright contained the line which was to become the cornerstone of Johnson's campaign, "Sound the Bugles Rumpsey, Dumpsey, Col. Johnson killed Tecumseh."

Richard Mentor Johnson quickly became the favorite of westerners, those in favor of hard money, and the urban working class. Various members of Jackson's Kitchen Cabinet supported his run as well, including Postmaster General Amos Kendall and Francis P. Blair, the editor of the *Washington Globe*, which served as the mouthpiece of the administration and the Democratic Party. Yet as the election grew nearer it was becoming obvious to many that Jackson and the party preferred Vice President Martin Van Buren. Some southern and western politicians though balked at the idea of the New York Democrat being in charge and suggested to Johnson that he run as a third party candidate. Johnson ultimately rejected these calls by David Crockett, John Bell, and others and focused his energies on securing the vice presidency instead.[233] Speaker Bell in fact had allegedly gone to great lengths to convince Johnson to help sabotage the upcoming convention in hopes of denying Van Buren the nomination. Crockett, Bell, White, and others had recently split from the party due to their opposition to the autocratic rule of Jackson.

The Democratic Party Convention opened on May 20, 1835, in Baltimore at the Fourth Presbyterian Church. There was no serious debate over the choice of Martin Van Buren to be the party's candidate, and in essence the meeting served more as coronation than a convention. The choice of running mate though proved to be much more contentious. Jackson supported Johnson due to the latter's war record and to his own fears of losing the western states to the Whigs. Yet despite the death of Julia Chinn a few years before, anger over Johnson's miscegenastic marriage, his current rumored relationships, rumors of corruption, and his stance on money, the bank, religion, and debtors left him questionable to many conservative delegates. Van Buren himself pondered whether Johnson could, "be relied upon to check the cupidity of his friends."[234] Virginia proved especially recalcitrant towards the nomination. One delegate questioned Johnson's commitment to the principles of the party, while others saw him as anathema to the slaveholders of the south.[235] The head of its delegation arose before the official count was given and stated that, "the Virginia delegation can in no wise recommend to the People of Virginia, for the office of Vice President, any individual who does not carry out or maintain the political principals Virginia ever held dear."[236] Also in agreement with Virginia was the Chief Justice of the Tennessee Supreme Court, John Catron, who wrote to Jackson questioning whether, "a lucky random shot, even if it did hit Tecumseh, qualifies a man for the Vice Presidency." Ironically, Jefferson had expressed a similar sentiment about Jackson years before. Further, Catron warned that the nomination of Johnson would expose to the nation, "that he had endeavored often to force his daughters into society, that the mother in her life time, and they now, rode in carriages, and claimed equality."[237]

As the delegates at the convention began to cast votes, it quickly emerged that Richard Johnson lacked the two thirds needed for the nomination. Virginia pushed its own choice, Sen. William Cabell Rives the former Ambassador to France and by now a bitter partisan of Jackson. Just then Joseph Holt, the Commonwealth's Attorney from Kentucky rose and gave an impassioned defense of Johnson that was described by one Democrat in attendance as, "one of the most eloquent and thrilling speeches that it has ever been my pleasure and privilege to listen to."[238] He described his fellow Kentuckian's, "scarred and shattered frame," as having a, "heart in all its recollections, its hopes, and its sympathies

... blended with the fortunes of the toiling millions ... the people love him because he loved them first."[239] He was in essence the next Andrew Jackson, warrior and Democrat, indeed much more so than Van Buren. The entire process came to a standstill until Sen. Silas Wright of New York grabbed a slave owning Tennessean named Edward Rucker from a local tavern and had him cast the state's votes as it had failed to send a delegation. A Vermont newspaper later remonstrated Rucker for having, "defeated the nomination of a white man as Vice-President," an action for which he was allegedly reward with a post office appointment.[240] With these additional 15 votes, Johnson was able to secure 178 delegates to Rives 87, one more than the 177 needed. He had been supported by the states of Vermont, New Hampshire, Massachusetts, Connecticut, Rhode Island, New York, Delaware, Pennsylvania, Tennessee, Kentucky, Ohio, Indiana, Mississippi, Louisiana, and Missouri. Both he and Van Buren were largely the choice of the north and west. Though the delegation from Virginia hissed loudly and promptly exited the hall, the deed was done, Richard Mentor Johnson was the Democratic nominee for the vice presidency.

In his acceptance speech given on May 23, 1835, Johnson highlighted his true Republican principles in terms of economic issues. Like many others of his party he had dabbled with certain Federalist/Whig economic policies following the War of 1812 out of, "patriotic necessity." Now a generation later, many of these actions and votes were being dredged up by his younger or more principled opponents to impugn his credentials. He reiterated the numerous times that he had stood against the idea of a national bank, even in the face of occasional Republican opposition. Yet, "the recent developments of the power of doing mischief possessed by a national bank, and the uncontrollable tendency to use this power to direct the politics of the country, have satisfied me that no such institution should be tolerated, under any circumstances." Likewise Johnson narrated how following the disastrous effects of the Dallas Tariff he became a staunch and perennial opponent of the concept. After wrapping up a further discussion of his stance against internal improvements, Johnson thanked the delegates for the, "confirmation, by the voice of my whole country, of the repeated proofs of approbation given by the people of my own state, to the well-meant labors of a life devoted to the service of the nation."[241]

The general election that followed was chaotic. The Whig Party, which had recently formed more in opposition to the rule of Jackson than around any principles, was more divided than even the Democrats. Four candidates emerged to challenge Van Buren, Sen. Daniel Webster in Massachusetts, Gen. William Henry Harrison in the north, Sen. Hugh L. Wright in the south, and Sen. Willie Mangum in South Carolina. Part of the Whig strategy was to steal enough states from Van Buren to have the election thrown into the House of Representatives where they hoped to have enough votes to deny the Democrats the presidency.

While Van Buren was attacked extensively by the Whig media, Johnson was also the subject of numerous scathing articles. His marriage to Julie Chinn and his current mistresses were used to damage the appeal of the Democratic ticket in the south. Referring to it as an amalgamation or worse in newspapers and in mailings, the Whigs neutralized much of Johnson's draw in the south and west. One newspaper jokingly commented on the Democrats assertion that, "Mr. Van Buren and Col. Johnson have no fellowship with political puritans and black legs," by asking, "how long since Col. Johnson conceived a dislike for black *legs?*"[242] The *State Journal* of Vermont alluded to his, "black ewe, which has produced him more, than all the black flocks have produced their owners in Tennessee."[243] Finally, the *Vermont Watchman* carried a story allegedly from a Kentucky periodical which related how, "Col. Johnson, returning recently in somewhat ill humor from an electioneering tour, undertook to inflict personal chastisement on his negro wife, for some misdemeanor of which she had been guilty."[244] According to their Kentucky source hysterical, vaudevillian chase developed between the two around his property. "We hope that scenes of this description will not often occur in the Colonel's household at Washington."[245] Cartoons helped to drive the point home to many and hinted at not only his notorious lifestyle but rumors of corruption as well.

The racial attacks against Johnson in fact began only a month after the ending of the Democratic Convention in 1835 when tales of Parthene's flight hit Whig newspapers. The death of his daughter Adaline during the campaign cycle, allegedly due to emotional stress from the attacks against her and her father, only further disheartened the nominee. In this he was suffering a similar fate to Jackson in 1828. At one point while he was campaigning in New York State, one of Johnson's slaves, and alleged brother-in-law, Marcellus Chinn, ran away. The Congressman spent much time and energy trying to regain his lost property/family member to the humor of the electorate.[246]

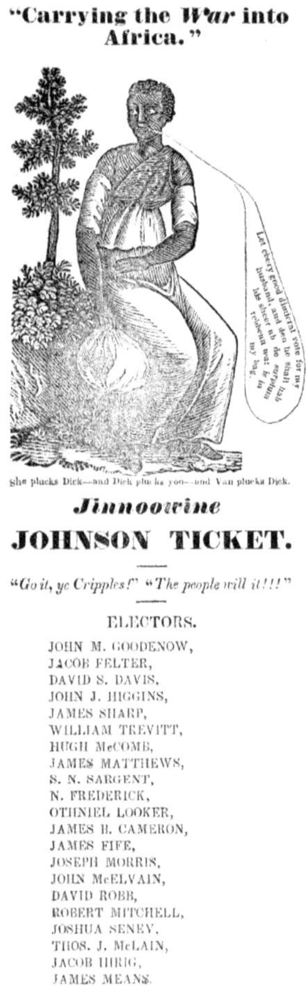
"Carrying the War into Africa."
Let ebery good dimicral vote for my husband, and den he shall hab de sheer ob de surplum rebbenu wat is in my bag.
She plucks Dick—and Dick plucks you—and Van plucks Dick.
Jinnoowine
JOHNSON TICKET.
"Go it, ye Cripples!" "The people will it!!!"
ELECTORS.
JOHN M. GOODENOW,
JACOB FELTER,
DAVID S. DAVIS,
JOHN J. HIGGINS,
JAMES SHARP,
WILLIAM TREVITT,
HUGH McCOMB,
JAMES MATTHEWS,
S. N. SARGENT,
N. FREDERICK,
OTHNIEL LOOKER,
JAMES B. CAMERON,
JAMES FIFE,
JOSEPH MORRIS,
JOHN McELVAIN,
DAVID ROBB,
ROBERT MITCHELL,
JOSHUA SENEY,
THOS. J. McLAIN,
JACOB IHRIG,
JAMES MEANS.

Image 10. Political Cartoon Showing Julia Chinn

All of these attacks coincided with the Snow Riot of August in 1835, a massive race riot which convulsed the capitol for weeks and reminded many southerners of the dangers of emancipation and amalgamation. Johnson himself was contacted by the owner of the slave who lay at the heart of the riot in an attempt to gain a pardon from Andrew Jackson.[247] Surely it was more than just his close friendship with the President that prompted Anna Thornton, the sympathetic slave owner, to enlist the Congressman's aid.

Nor were racially charged invectives leveled only against Johnson. The *Burlington Free Press* reported in September 1836 that, "a Van Buren newspaper, called the 'Chickasaw Union,' has been started at Pontotoc, Mississippi. It is evidently conducted by an association of Chickasaws. The Indians are for Mr. Van Buren, the negroes for Col. Johnson, and the white folks for Gen. Harrison."[248] Racial politics were hardly just confined to the south or the Democratic Party.

The Anti-Masonic Party, which had arisen in the late 1820s due to the Morgan Affair, threw their weight firmly behind the Whig candidates. Johnson was personally attacked for being an adherent of the Free Masons and a member of the Grand Chapter of Kentucky since at least 1824. Though they may have approved of his democratic principles and those of Van Buren, they lamented that there was no way the latter would run without, "Col. Johnson on his back," thus dooming the ticket.[249] As one of the platforms of the Van Buren ticket was, "uncompromising opposition to all combinations and associations, whether secret or public," many of the potential Democratic voters demurred, associating Free Masonry with Federalism and aristocratic principles. "The freemasonry of this man makes him dear to the aristocracy."[250]

The Whigs were also quick to address the issues of Johnson's historical simony. Rumors spread that despite his opposition to an organized, national bank he was more than willing to accept campaign contributions from the various "pet" banks set up after Jackson's withdrawal of state funds from the Bank of the United States. These allegations against both him and others even led to a Congressional investigation. "A pet in Baltimore has replied to the written inquires which the committee made, and among other facts, states, that they recently made a loan of six thousand dollars, to the Hon. R.M. Johnson."[251] The larger issue though for many Whigs was the emerging hereditary nature of the presidency. "If Gen. Jackson can appoint Mr. Van Buren his successor to the Presidential chair, why may not Mr. Van Buren, in like manner, appoint Col. Richard M. Johnson?"[252] The Federalists had already lived through this with the succession of leaders from Jefferson to Monroe and feared a repetition.

Democratic newspapers were quick to not only support Johnson but also to denounce those within the party who disparaged him. "It seems that Col. Johnson does not suit the refined notions of our dandy nobility … The poor man's friend, the faithful public servant, the patriot, who spilt his blood and periled his life in defence of his country, who saved the women of the West from the savage scalping knife, and the brutality of the British soldiary."[253] Johnson himself went after Rep. Francis Granger, the running mate of both Harrison and Webster, accusing him of being, "an abolitionist, that he was an organ of that party, and that he maintained abolition principles and opinions on the floor of congress last winter."[254] Though these attacks were largely baseless they would serve to damage Granger's appeal in the south. At the same time Harrison and White were accused of being abolitionists and nullifiers, respectively, again false charges.

Oliver C. Comstock, a Baptist minister and former member of the House from New York, became one of the staunchest defenders of Johnson's character. A newspaper lambasted him as the man who "whitewashed a dark spot in Col. Johnson's character."[255] For his efforts he was elected to be Chaplain of the House of Representatives, serving for a few months until the ending of the 24th Congress in March 1837 before leaving the office. Likewise the famed evangelist Walter Scott published a story of an encounter with Richard and his brother John Telemachus in his magazine *Evangelist* in 1835.

Finally, even the hero's war record became a tool of both campaigns. Democratic newspapers were quick to point out and highlight the actions of the hero of the Thames. "The battle of the Thames was won by colonel Johnson without Harrison's knowledge or orders."[256] While at the same time Whig periodicals pointed to Harrison's dominant role in both the campaign and battle, Johnson's slaying of Tecumseh was questioned, and the Colonel's own praise of Harrison in 1813 and 1814 was resurrected and used against him.

As presidential candidates did not actively seek to run for office at the time, Van Buren's delegates in general and Johnson in particular crisscrossed the nation seeking to garner support and votes. Johnson tended to remain within his home state, attending various events and dinners. In October 1836 alone, the Colonel spoke to a packed courthouse in Franklin, was the guest of honor at a dinner in Flemingsburg, and gave a speech in Henry County. That same month an anniversary celebration of the Battle of the Thames was thrown in Mercer County with Johnson as the guest of honor. The fact that he was spending so much time in his home state seemed to indicate that the Democrats foresaw a tough battle there. Yet overall the Democrats ran a much more positive campaign than the Whigs. Attacks on Harrison and the other candidates tended to be less personal and more substance based. As one party paper opined ...

> "It seems to us strange, that after all the experiences, since the establishment of our Republic, it is not better known by editors generally, that all bitter and criminating accusations against candidates for office, only tend to elicit inquiry and enlist more in their favor than would otherwise have supported them- thus increasing instead of diminishing their chances of success. The whig papers are working admirably, in their current publications respecting Mr. Johnson and his children, to help him to the vice presidency!"[257]

In the end, Van Buren managed to gather 170 electoral votes and 50.8% of the popular to the combined 124 of the Whigs. Yet in a telling result the Democrats failed to carry the majority of the old Northwestern Territory and three southern states. Johnson himself was unable to deliver his home state to Van Buren, a situation that had only happened three times before in the previous half century.[258] Though the Democrats had managed to surpass Jackson's total popular vote from 1832, so had the Whigs. Van Buren did not receive a clear mandate from the people.

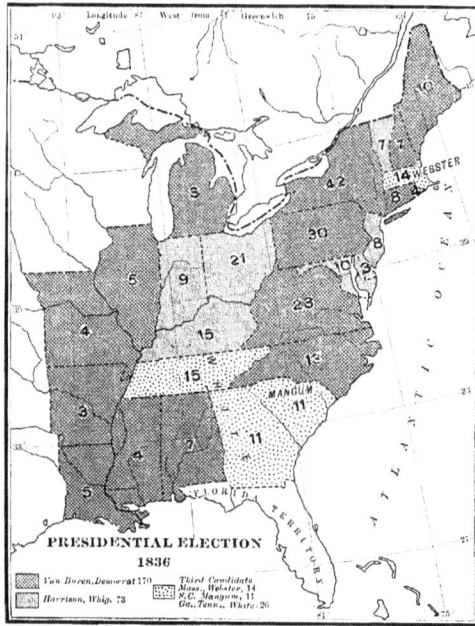

Image 11. The Election of 1836

Yet the chaos of the election did not stop there. The Virginia slate of electors, though voting for Van Buren, refused to vote for Johnson as well. Casting all of its 23 votes for William Smith, the former senator from South Carolina, Virginia deprived Johnson by two votes of the vice presidency. Under the terms of the XII Amendment, the vice presidential election was then thrown into the Senate between the top two vote getters, Rep. Richard Mentor Johnson and Rep. Francis Granger. There was little doubt as to the outcome of this secondary election as it was clear that the Senate would go for the, "Patriot Soldier, the Philanthropist, the friend of the Poor, and the defender of the Rich."[259] Yet various Whig newspapers continued to press the issue home in the weeks before the vote in the Senate, alternating between attacks upon the undemocratic nature of the process and assaults on Johnson's character.

"He is not a man of strict and stern integrity. He has been charged with being a swindler-of defrauding banks of large sums, of still being indebted to them, and avoiding payment ... He is not a man of intellect ... He is content to be considered the successful hero who met the savage Tecumseh in single combat, and slew him, when he knows full well that Julius Caesar has as good a claim as he, to the honor of that might deed. His whole fame rests on this achievement, the Sunday Mail Report, and an annual speech on imprisonment for debt, manufactured by whom, heaven only knows ... his mental energies undisciplined- his fancies uncultivated- his tastes groveling."[260]

In the end, it took only a single ballot that resulted in a party line 33-16 vote to finally give Johnson the vice presidency, a message had been sent. His own home state of Kentucky, represented by Whig Senators Clay and Crittenden in fact duly voted against him. Yet despite this, once the election was decided a spirit of reconciliation temporarily settled upon the nation. Even the virulent anti-Democratic newspaper, the *New York Star,* published a lengthy apology piece in January 1837 seeking to correct the record on the racial charges against him. In the end, the Colonel could look back at his meteoric rise and look forward as well to what could be in the future.

Chapter VI

Vice President Rumpsey Dumpsey

The position of Vice President has perhaps best been described as, "not worth a bucket of warm piss." It was often a lonely, thankless position frequently filled for political reasons that were just as soon forgotten once the ticket won in November. Richard Mentor Johnson certainly discovered this to be true upon taking the oath of office from William Rufus King in March 1837. Yet in the end he was able to make his mark upon that, "respectable and ... exalted," office in a variety of interesting ways.[261]

It was not uncommon for a President at this time to not deal directly or frequently with their Vice President. Often time running mates were chosen for political or geographic reasons that did not reflect any ability to work productively together between the two men. Adams and Jefferson perfectly exemplified this from 1797 to 1801 as did Calhoun with both John Q. Adams and Jackson from 1825 to 1832. Besides their constitutional duty of overseeing the Senate, the majority of Vice Presidents passed their four years in relative obscurity. Many hoped to position themselves for a run as President, though except in the cases of Adams, Jefferson, and Van Buren, this was rarely successful.

In the above regard, Johnson was no different than previous Vice Presidents. He had a cordial relationship with President Van Buren but was rarely if ever consulted on any policy matters. The President's agenda was instead pushed by William Rufus King, the President pro tempore, and Johnson confined himself to merely running the Senate. In this he was perhaps happiest as it was familiar territory. Yet with a Democratic supermajority in place, there seemed to be little for him to do besides chat cordially with members around one of the fireplaces in the chamber. By all accounts he was an impartial President of the Senate and was praised by Henry Clay and other Whigs upon his departure in 1841, a far cry from the treatment of Calhoun a few years before. Yet he was also not exceptionally skilled at his position, with one newspaper describing the situation as, "the Colonel was 'not at home,' and in a most uncomfortable berth, which the country has given him. However excellent the Colonel may have been in 'injun-killing,' it is quite clear, his gun will go amiss in settling points of order."[262] Likewise by the end of his first year in office a newspaper noticed that few people even visited upon Johnson at his home, and when they did they made sure to visit when they knew the Senate would be in session.[263]

Concerns were early on raised by the Whig press about his commitment to a new Bank of the United States. Beyond the typical mudslinging of the press, these questions arose due to his past support for the institution in the immediate aftermath of the War of 1812. In an effort to quite the storm Johnson disseminated a letter to friendly newspaper outlets in July 1837 in which he asked the public to, "judge me by my works, you may know that the paragraph is without a shadow of foundation ... I have sustained, and I intend to sustain, the Administration of the General Government, in the course which it has pursued."[264] Despite his denials, the first major piece of legislation proposed by Pres. Van Buren only served to further raise questions about his views, especially among members of the Locofocos wing of the Democratic Party.

Perhaps Johnson's most important moment as President of the Senate came on September 4, 1837, as he gaveled in a special session of Congress. The Panic of 1837 was firmly gripping the nation and Van Buren called the various Senators and Representatives to the capital to take action on his proposal for an independent treasury. Yet the issue was so decisive within his own party that it would not be passed until 1840. Johnson was called upon as the presiding officer of the Senate to appoint a committee to investigate the plan. He became the first Vice President to exercise this power since it was stripped away following Calhoun's apparent abuse of it 12 years before. Johnson's action was seen as a necessity due to the fact that the, "extra session of Congress (was) called for a special purpose, and it was not expected that matters of general legislation would be brought forward."[265] Yet Whig papers were quick to pounce on this statement, asking, "Very proper! But what does he think of the Bank?"[266] Yet despite the attacks of the opposition Johnson never expressed any serious intentions to revive the defunct institution. Van Buren's insistence on an independent treasury, however, did not sit well with all Democrat voters.

In terms of foreign affairs, the most pressing issue confronting the Van Buren White House was the Caroline Affair of late 1837. A series of rebellions had erupted in Canada that year aimed at acquiring greater self-rule for the colony. A certain amount of sympathy existed among many northern Americans for this cause and volunteers, money, supplies, and weapons began to flow across the porous border. In response to these moves, in December 1837 British authorities crossed the border, seized the ship *Caroline*, lit her on fire, and pushed her over Niagara Falls, killing one American in the process. Coming a generation after the ending of the War of 1812, many Americans howled for war as the press exaggerated the details of the incident. Though Van Buren sought peace, deploying Gen. Winfield Scott on the border to prevent further incursions by either side, attacking Patriot elements within the nation, and beginning the process of negotiating with the British, the position of Vice President Johnson is more difficult to pin down.

As a veteran of the War of 1812, an Anglophobe, and a staunch supporter of democracy one would imagine Johnson to be at least sympathetic to the Patriot cause. In 1841, the *New York Tribune* reported that a Patriot delegation in the state to raise funds claimed it had, "covert assistance," from the U.S. government. In addition, the Canadians alleged that, "the 'patriot' cause was now headed by Col. Johnson."[267] The Vice President had in fact made a trip to New York state in November 1837 on the eve of the Caroline Affair. While we do not have any active statements from the Vice President on the rebellion or the Patriot movement, we can assume that if not openly supportive of it, he was at least personally in favor of the cause.

As mentioned above, Vice President Johnson did take an extended trip to New York City in the late fall of 1837. He arrived on the morning of November 14 and despite a heavy snowstorm, was met by a throng of well-wishers. He stayed at the Washington Hotel on Broadway across from Bowling Green, the former headquarters of the General during the American Revolution, and was treated to a number of dinners. On December 2 he was, "toasted about the streets, preceded by a small company of infantry and a few horsemen, and followed by his friends in two carriages."[268] Amused Manhattan pedestrians stopped at the sounds of a fife and drum but generally ignored the parade. Part of his trip was also occupied by his sitting for a bust as well as a visit from his former opponent, Rep. Francis Granger. After remaining in New York City almost three weeks, Johnson took his leave by boat to Philadelphia on the evening of December 4. Escorted by a couple of freemasons, 20 infantrymen, and six cavalry he proceeded to the city docks while several cannons set up on the Battery fired off a salute and his small martial escort played the popular, and ironic song, "To the Girl I Left Behind Me."

A few interesting notes did emerge during his time in office. He took to wearing a scarlet vest and bowtie daily for years; items of regalia that became trademark of Richard Mentor Johnson. According to traditions the Vice President was walking with James Reeside in the capital when the latter passed a men's shop and admired a red vest inside. Johnson suggested to Reeside that he purchase it as it matched the colors of his stagecoach service. His friend replied that he would if Johnson did as well. Since that time Vice President Johnson was easily recognizable around town in his signature accessory. Newspapers still reported his wearing of the garment over a decade later in the last year of his life. "Col. Richard M. Johnson has gone to Washington city on private business ... He wore the red vest."[269] In addition, his last few months in office saw the first major filibuster undertaken in American legislative history as William Rufus King sought to kill Clay's sponsorship of the Third Bank of the United States and a rule change to the Senate to allow the majority party to push through laws and votes.

Vice President Johnson also became known for the sheer number of tie-breaking votes he was required to cast as President of the Senate. It is surprising that this was necessary given the overwhelming Democratic presence within Congress. Yet dissension within the party's ranks over issues of slavery and the President's disastrous handling of the Panic of 1837 led to many close and controversial votes. Johnson would go on to cast 17 tie breaking votes during his four years in office, making him fourth in American history behind John Adams (29) John C. Calhoun (28), and George Dallas (19). Yet one should consider that

Adams and Calhoun served two terms while Dallas and Johnson only served one, making the feat that much more impressive. Many of these regarded procedural issues of his age old interest in the granting of relief to aged veterans or their descendants. To quote Johnson, he quite often, "used my humble abilities in favor of those laws which have extended compensation to the officers and soldiers who have bravely fought, and freely bled, in their country's cause, and to widows and orphans of those who perished."[270] Yet besides this spirited defense to the people of Kentucky, he rarely gave any other statement to the Senate as had his predecessor to explain his vote. His most important vote occurred regarding a major treaty with the Six Nations in March 1840. The Treaty of Buffalo Creek signed in January 1838 continued the process begun by the Indian Removal Act and made famous by the Trail of Tears by moving more Iroquois to Kansas. The Six Nations had been slowly losing lands around the Great Lakes since the middle of the eighteenth century including following the Treaty of Ft. Stanwix in 1784, the original of which was incidentally recorded as being in Johnson's personal possession in the 1830s.[271] Johnson continued the more aggressive Jacksonian policy towards Natives east of the Mississippi by casting the tie breaking vote to push the Indians out despite the reservations of many that the signatures of the Indians were obtained by less than honorable means.

Johnson also continued the politics of personal relationships and patronage that had characterized his time in the House. Despite his earlier vehement stance against collusions between church and state, his belief in patronage and personal religious ties got the better of him when he requested relief for a Baptist church in Washington.[272] He forwarded petitions to promote friends and family members while at the same time denying those which conflicted with his interests. An example of the latter was his rejection of a petition by Lewis Tappan of Amistad Case fame for the abolition of slavery in Washington as well as the territories. Johnson eloquently couched his refusal in his belief in state's rights, arguing that the citizens of one polity cannot force their views upon another and that it was his job as President of the Senate to prevent such a thing from occurring. "If a number of citizens should consider a republican government a grievance and petition Congress to establish a monarchy ... I should not consider it my duty to present their petitions to the Senate, nor do I consider it my duty to present a petition, the certain tendency of which is to destroy the harmony and eventually break asunder the bonds of our Union."[273]

Yet Johnson's personal life began to slowly unravel shortly after assuming his post. The death of his wife and daughter as well as the numerous personal attacks against him slowly took their toll on his bearing and health. Always in financial constraints, the Panic of 1837 further heavily damaged him economically. In 1838, he and four other defendants went into default over a promissory note of $3,000 from the Commonwealth Bank of Boston and were ruled against by the state court. As late as 1840 he became the subject of a lawsuit by Richard Menefee, the famed, young Kentucky Whig, and along with David Sayre was forced to pay $2,300.[274] This despite the fact that his annual salary, at $5,000 a year, was around 16 times what a typical factory worker at the time would make. In addition, it came out years later that he had received $18,000 in a questionable, if not illegal, land deal during his time in office in which he used his political influence to push for the funding of Capt. Simeon Buckner in a scheme to transport the Chickasaw by boat to reservations.[275] It was further revealed by the Stuart Report in 1842 that this particular episode cost the government $122,000 as not only was the relocation handled in an inefficient manner but also that the vast majority of Indians simply chose to travel by land.[276]

Johnson took a nine-month leave from the Senate to return to his plantation in Kentucky. Here, he sought to straighten out his finances which he hoped to augment by constructing a spa and a tavern on his property. The scarlet vested Vice President of the nation then settled down to tending bar for visitors to his establishment. Amos Kendall in a report to the President commented on the way in which the Vice President even gave his, "personal superintendence to the chicken and egg purchasing and watermelon selling department."[277] He went on to describe how, "the old gentleman seems to enjoy the business of *Tavern-Keeping* as well as any host I ever stopped with ... the example of Cincinnatus laying down his public honors and returning to his plough should no longer be quoted as worthy of imitation, when the Vice President of these United States, with all his civic and military honors clustered around his time honored brow, is, or seems to be so happy in the inglorious pursuit of tavern keeping."[278] While it was not odd for a Vice President to tend to other affairs during his time in office, the amount of time that Johnson left for and his actions during it were certainly bizarre.

Reoccurring illnesses likewise began to detract from his countenance leaving him shabby and short-tempered, especially when compared to the friendly and immaculately dressed Van Buren. An English traveler, Harriet Martineau, recorded that, "if he should become President, he will be as strange- looking a potentate as ever ruled. His countenance is wild, though with much cleverness in it; his hair wanders all abroad, and he wears no cravat. But there is no telling how he might look if he dressed like other people."[279] Whig periodicals were likewise quick to highlight any mistake made by the man while presiding over the Senate.

> "The Colonel, who is the most awkward and inefficient presiding officer, became greatly embarrassed when a certain bill was ordered to be engrossed and read a third time. He rose and said—'Senators, it is moved-and-and seconded-that the-bill-that the bill'—and here he stuck fast. A short pause ensued, when Mr. Calhoun cried out, 'be engrossed and read a third time,' in a tone of sharp and fiery impatience that made Col. Johnson start back in his seat and set the whole Senate into a titter."[280]

Johnson also spent considerable energy on his other pastime, gathering federal funding for him or his relatives. Education had long been an interest of the Vice President as it had been for his father in Kentucky during the 1790s and 1800s. This can be seen through an 1821 bill he introduced to the House to charter Columbian College in Washington, modern day George Washington University as well as through the efforts he undertook to insure the education of his daughters. Not surprisingly therefore, perhaps the longest felt contribution of Johnson was his sponsorship of a school for local Indians.

As has been previously touched upon, the Baptist church in Kentucky at the time was becoming heavily involved in the issue of education.

Numerous schools including Transylvania University, Bacon College, and Rittenhouse Academy had been established in the area under the auspices of the Baptist faith. As early as 1817 Johnson and Thomas Lorraine McKenney were exchanging letters discussing the possibility of educating the Natives in order to civilize them.[281] A few years later McKenney and Johnson began discussing the logistics of such an endeavor, stating as its aim ...

> "to gain permission from the Indians of the different tribes ... to have three, four, or more, children from a tribe brought into this country (Kentucky) for education—the children to be bought, fed, clothed, and educated at the expense, and under the care and direction of the society—to be taught reading, writing, and arithmetic; and in some cases, where genius warrants it, the higher branches of literature; to make the boys acquainted with husbandry, and the girls with domestic employment."[282]

Overall, the theory behind the school was one of turnkey education. The students upon graduation would return to their villages, "to instruct their other children at their respective towns."[283] Additional schools can be constructed by the Natives in order to transform their own societies from within. The Quaker McKenney would go on to become the first Superintendent of Indian Affairs and long championed both the education and the civilization, rather than extermination, of the tribes.

His connection with the institution began in 1825 following a treaty made between the American government and the Choctaw nation which included a provision for the education of their youth. Johnson, a Representative at the time, wrote to Sec. of War James Barbour offering his land and services for the proposed school. As this was largely a project of the Baptist church, the Johnson family became naturally involved.[284]

> "I have a house with 3 rooms 20×30 feet which I shall appropriate exclusively to their accommodation. I have another house with four Rooms 20 feet square which

will do for the Teacher to live in & one room for the school—the whole establishment will be within my own fences so that no time shall be lost; the Indians will be here by the 15th of Oct. I am now preparing to receive them—my workmen are fixing Tables, Benches, Chairs &&. I have engaged a Teacher of uncommon merit—a scientific character, and in the habit of Teaching from the ABC he is a man of moral character; a Preacher of the gospel, of industrious habits and dignified manners. I shall have all things ready to receive them by the 12th of next month or sooner—We shall have as many white children to be taught with them to learn them to speak the English Language as well as to learn them to read &&&.

"During my stay at home each year I shall devote much of my time towards establishing to them habits that will govern them through life ... I intend to have them well fed, well clothed & well educated ... I would rather a gross sum would be allowed for each scholar per annum to Include every expense so as to have no contingencies ... I shall see that a faithful part is done the Indians ... It will not do to extend any more patronage to the Schools in that nation—they have appropriated other funds to those missionary schools & they do not see the benefit that I know will result to this place. We shall have trustees appointed to report the progress from time to time."[285]

Peter Pitchlynn of the Choctaw Tribe, also known as Snapping Turtle, served as that group's representative for the project. Pitchlynn himself had been educated at various American schools in Tennessee and was a firm believer in the value of education as a way to modernize and advance the Native people.

Johnson did devote considerable time and energy to the academy, though undoubtedly the money that it brought in from the federal government proved an impetus to his actions. The institution was quickly up and running as Lafayette is recorded as having toured it during his time in Kentucky that same year. From the first 21 boys who arrived around November 1825, the school grew to host an average class size of between 200 and 300. Each boy was re-christened with the name of an American statesman. The school rolls therefore read like a who's who of national politics in the 1830s with such names as Andrew Jackson, Henry Clay, Richard Rush, James Barbour, and of course Richard Johnson.[286]

The local Indians apparently responded favorably to the establishment of the academy as enrollment quickly picked up. Johnson pledged himself towards perfecting the school but also constantly pressed his fellow Congressmen for more funding.

> "This shall be equal to any school in the U. States & I pledge myself that ample justice shall be done to every Boy ... It is in your power to do more to enlighten the Indians by encouraging this school than any man in the world—loose not the opportunity ... Mr. Ward informs me that some feeble opposition was made to sending the 36 Boys because of the expence. If any letter is written to you on that subject from any malcontent please place the matter on its proper footing. We are not allowed a liberal price by any means. We ought to have more."[287]

Though Peter Pitchlynn wrote a scathing expose on conditions in the school in 1828, Johnson quickly confronted the allegations publically, protesting his innocence. He must have been largely vindicated, or was at least better connected than Pitchlynn, as the institution continued to thrive and grow for years. A report by Robert Ould, who arrived in 1828 to reorganize the school along the lines of the latest educational pedagogy, reported the following to the Secretary of War ...

> "In conformity to instructions I repaired to the Choctaw Academy situated on the Bank of Elkhorn a beautiful stream in Scott County near the residence of Colonel Richard M. Johnson for the purpose of placing that interesting Institution upon the Lancasterian System

which has been done it is believed both to the satisfaction of the Superintendent and pupils. I cannot close this report without adverting to the great and rapid progress of the scholars together with their decent and orderly appearance being generally healthy, contented, obedient and clean in their clothing, comfortable in their accommodations and large and commodious buildings for the School and for Lodging. Nor can I omit to mention in this report the interesting fact that many of these youths have made an open and public profession of religion being regular members of the sundry respectable denominations which prevail in that neighborhood—nor does their profession outstrip their practice for I was witness to many traits of character truly delightful ... this Institution at once (and I hope for ever) sets aside the old and musty idea that the sons of the forest are incapable of civilization."[288]

As the nation attempted to pacify additional tribes, Johnson was quick to volunteer his academy for their youth. In 1828, he inquired as to the possibility of Cherokee youth, then in the process of being expelled from the south, being sent to Blue Springs as well. In gratitude Opo-tho-lo-hola, an Indian chief, named his son "Richard Mentor Johnson" and sent him to Kentucky to be educated.[289] The expanding school was relocated in 1831 to White Sulphur Spring, also owned by Johnson, and continued to turn out chiefs, Protestant preachers, and men who helped to modernize their tribes. One of its most famous graduates was his own nephew, Robert Ward Johnson who would go on to become a member of "the Family" and one of the most powerful men in Arkansas politics during 1850s and 1860s.

Yet Johnson's scandalous background when combined with his lack of appeal to conservative and southern voters led the party to consider dropping him in the 1840 election. One paper summarized the view of many that the party was looking elsewhere as, "now that he can be no farther use in forwarding the progress of their political intrigues."[290] The Panic of 1837 had seriously crippled the Democratic Party as a brand. The Vice President himself, despite his best efforts to, "not let the Whigs get HIS district," failed to even deliver his own district back in Kentucky during the 1837 election cycle.[291] This seat had been held by a Johnson, save for a three-year period, from 1807 to 1833. As early as September 1838, rumors were already beginning to float in newspapers that in order to secure the conservative vote Van Buren was going to abandon his Vice President for Rep. Francis Rives of Virginia.[292] Other names also began to be tossed around, including the champion of Manifest Destiny Thomas Hart Benton of Missouri, Sec. of State John Forsyth from Georgia, James Buchanan of Pennsylvania, and Ambassador Andrew Stevenson of Virginia. Even his mentor and one time ardent supporter Andrew Jackson cast about for other candidates, most notably James K. Polk of Tennessee. The former President wrote to Francis P. Blair shortly before the convention stating his position as, "I like Col. Johnson but I like my country more, and I allway go for my Country first, and then for my friend."[293] The Locofocos also allegedly attempted to distance themselves from his candidacy, though this may have been more of a general rebuke against Van Buren's failure to aid the common workingman. An effort was even made to suggest that the decision was the Vice President's, alleging that he was desirous seeking the governorship of Kentucky instead.

Johnson himself attempted to confront these concerns head on in a letter that was released to the press in June 1839. In a similar line of thinking to many before him and since, he states that, "the office of vice president is one that should not be sought," it is merely an honor bestowed upon the individual by the people. For Johnson it was, "a testimony of approbation of my public services, and as a mark of their highest confidence in my fidelity and political principles." If the people choose to return him to office he would do so willingly, however, if the party went with another candidate, "I shall manifest as much cheerfulness in retiring from the service of the people as I have to serve them when they have requested it."[294] Yet not all were convinced of the motives of this self-proclaimed modern day Cincinnatus. "The grand amalgamator of the Great Crossings finds five thousand a year and the privilege of snoozing in the Senate chamber to pleasant to be given (up)."[295] The *Maumee City Express* recommended that if Johnson was looking for a position better suited to his talents, perhaps he should consider being named minister to the, "fair court," of Haiti.[296]

Pres. Van Buren initially preferred to keep Johnson, hoping to utilize his appeal to veterans and hard money enthusiasts, yet his declining appeal, especially in the west, began to make this an untenable move. Col. Johnson delivered a letter to the assembled Democratic Convention, again assembled at Baltimore, in April 1840 expressing his desires to once again seek the nomination. "I will be perfectly satisfied with the course the Convention shall adopt; and, in any event, must beg of them not to suffer any feelings of partiality for me to endanger the principles which we are united in sustaining ... in a Republic no citizen has any claims upon the people to election to any office."[297] Johnson goes on to state that any elected office should not be seen as a reward for past service, as the service should have been done simply for the good of the nation. He would serve if called upon, but sought neither wreaths of victory nor robes of office. In reality, his surrogates were hard at work seeking to secure his candidacy against several notable opponents. Yet in the end an unsure and unconvinced Democratic Party gave him only 99 votes with 132 delegates aligning against him. Included in the latter number were 42 officials from Van Buren's own home state, a telling move considering the President's influence over that delegation. The convention then moved to allow each state to nominate their own candidate for Vice President rather than risking committing to or against Johnson. Many observers were left to wonder, "what has Col. Johnson done that he is not as worthy of re-election as Martin Van Buren."[298] The move though was prompted more by Van Buren's weakness than Johnson's flaws. In a repetition of the Whig's tactic from four years before, the Democrats hoped to bolster Van Buren's chances with a series of local sons as his running mates. The hope was to patch together enough electoral votes for the presidency and then have the vice presidential election thrown into the Senate as it had been in 1836. Though this move may have benefited Van Buren, it portended poorly for Johnson. In fact many southern states actually preferred John Tyler of Virginia, an erstwhile conservative Democrat drafted by the Whigs to join the Harrison ticket to Richard Mentor Johnson. In late May 1840, the Locofocos faction of the party assembled but likewise failed to nominate a candidate. Martin Van Buren remains the only candidate in the last two centuries since the adoption of the XII Amendment to run without an official running mate.

For his part, Johnson was rightly offended by the move. He was described shortly afterwards as a, "wronged man," with the press mocking the sympathetic condolences of his fellow party members. "Col. Johnson, a good and easy soul as he is, is not aware of all the artifices of the political hucksters about him. The scales however, are falling from his eyes, and ere long he will see his friends without the aid of his telescope."[299] Soon afterwards the Vice President left his dwelling in Washington and returned to Kentucky, a disillusioned man. Talk even emerged of him supporting Harrison in the coming contest. Rumors spread of him quarrelling with Van Buren, blaming the Little Magician of engineering his failed nomination. Likewise he was said to have almost come to blows with Sen. Thomas H. Benton of Missouri after the latter disparaged Gen. Harrison in his presence, though Johnson himself denied the affair a few weeks later in a letter.[300] A similar story emerged in July while the Vice President was on a visit to New York City. He was greeted by an ovation at the Bowery Theater upon entering his box which was followed by, "some 'British' alien," who offered three groans for Harrison. Col. Johnson, "sprang from his seat ... his eyes flashing fire that such an insu insult should be offered in his presence, his lips parted as if he would have spoken- but it was needless: for the glow of patriotism that animated him found place in every man's bosom in the place, and heartfelt cheers and shouts arose."[301]

Yet the undemocratic nature of the process angered many, and while Virginia, Massachusetts, and Tennessee seized upon Gov. Polk of Tennessee, New York, Pennsylvania, Ohio, Kentucky, Indiana, Illinois, Michigan, Missouri and a few other states quickly chose Johnson as their candidate anyway due to his popularity with the urban, working class. A leading Pennsylvania Democratic paper wrote in December 1839 that Johnson was the choice of the masses, surpassed only by Jackson in terms of service to the country on the battlefield and by no one in terms of his legislative accomplishments. "Van Buren, Johnson, and Porter form a tower of strength against which the storm of federalism may beat in vein."[302] Arkansas went so far as to threaten to vote for Harrison should Johnson not be on the ticket.[303] As no other credible Democrat emerged, Johnson soon took to actively campaigning for a Van Buren-Johnson ticket. He reminded voters of his efforts both on the battlefield and in Congress, dramatically tearing open his shirt at one point while stumping in Ohio to show his scars from the Thames. Shortly afterwards while giving a speech in Columbus he attacked the Whigs for attempting to force a monarchy on the country. Apparently his speaking style while in that state grew so inflammatory towards native son William Henry Harrison, possibly to make up for his own words of praise for the General from 1813 that were being resurrected and used against him, that a small-scale riot was touched off in Cleveland.[304] From there he traveled to Detroit to attend a barbeque at the farm of former governor and Secretary of War Lewis Cass, himself the Democratic candidate for President in 1848. The Vice President also retained his loyal cadre of supporters. In late November 1838, when famed abolitionist Rev. Nathaniel Colver of the Baptist church in Redding, Connecticut accused Johnson of not only bearing children with an African, but, "of making merchandize of the offspring of his own loins, of selling his own sons and daughters into slavery," a group of local Democrats responded by blowing up the church during the early hours of the next morning with a barrel of gunpowder placed under the pulpit.[305] "The pulpit was demolished, the front of the building displaced several feet, the windows broken out, and the walls destroyed."[306]

As shown by the speech of Rev. Colver, at the time politicians' children were not exempt from being used as political fodder during a campaign. A Whig newspaper in 1839 joked that, "one of Richard M. Johnson's daughters bears the name of Alice. It wouldn't do to sing 'Alice Gray' to her, for it would be the wrong color."[307] Another wrote that it was quite alright for Johnson to have a kink or two in his head as, "his wife has a thousand."[308] The Vermont newspaper, *The Voice of Freedom*, published the following scandalous story in August 1839 ...

> *Most Alarming Outrage!* His Honor Richard M. Johnson, Vice President of the United States, on a recent excursion with his two accomplished daughters, took a short residence at Tuscaloosa. The fair ones whose complexion was not liable to injury from exposure to the sun, were much prone to promenade the street, displaying the brilliant jewels and rich paraphernalia which as the daughter of the second officer of the United States they felt entitled to wear.

One afternoon while there, the Vice President being particularly engaged, the young ladies with his leave ventured out without a protector, purposing to return in an hour. The hour elapsed-another-and another, the ladies did not appear. The tea table was prepared- but the darlings appeared not to grace the table. His honor becoming alarmed for their safety despatched messengers and went himself immediately in search. Long and unwearied was the search, until, about two days after, they were found on a sugar plantation, busily and laboriously employed with a hundred others, under the care of a master!

The indignant father was ready to serve upon the manager the fate of Tecumseh- when two loafers stepped up and told him to beware. We, said the loafers, are the men who have seized your daughters, and we have done it *legally* too: if you doubt it, read this seventh section of a law of Alabama, passed last February.

"Any person may seize upon and make a *slave for life any free person of color* who may be found in this State after the passage of this act, and who shall have come to this State since its passage."

The Vice President was dumbfounded! Here was the law- and there was his daughters in servitude! There was but one recourse and he applied to the owner to know the price.

"A thousand dollars apiece- as they are rather slender."

The two thousands were paid- a bill of sale taken, and the ebony jewels restored to the cabinet!

[The above circumstances have not yet taken place, but should the Vice President enter into Alabama with his family, the law of that State would give full countenance to such proceedings][309]

The Vice President's personal life became as much a target for the Whigs as had been the relationships of Jackson and Jefferson before him. Though several prominent Democratic papers attempted to similarly tarnish Harrison's image by suggesting that he had several mixed breed children of his own by a Native woman, for a variety of reasons the stories gained less traction.[310]

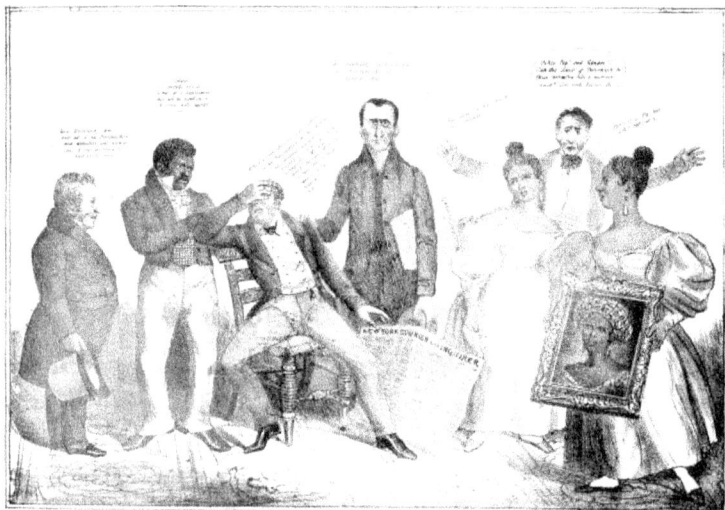

AN AFFECTING SCENE IN KENTUCKY.

Image 12. Political Cartoon Depicting Johnson with His Daughters Holding a Picture of Julia Chinn

In a repetition of the situation in 1836 Johnson's "father-in-law," Daniel Chinn, fled to Canada as the Vice President was stumping in Detroit. Despite his best efforts, pleading letters, implied threats, and the assistance of slave catchers he was never able to get his property back.[311] Occurring so close as it was to the site of his famous victory must have been doubly hard on Johnson. Infighting within the party proved as well to be costly, with commentators at the time opining on the lackluster use of Johnson in western and southern states.[312] John C. Calhoun expressed the view of many southerners in proclaiming that, "in no event ought we to vote for Johnson, unless our vote should be the casting vote; but in that case, we ought, as bitter as would be the pill."[313]

Famed Baltimore author Edgar Allen Poe penned a short story in 1839 entitled, "The Man That Was Used Up: A Tale of the Late Bugaboo and Kickapoo Campaign." The premise of the story revolves around a military hero named Gen. John A.B.C. Smith who was renowned for his heroism in battle, the scars he received fighting Indians, and his popularity with the masses. Yet in the end it is revealed that he is more machine than man, a used up man kept relevant only by his scars. While many have opined for years that Poe meant his character to be Gen. Winfield Scott, the similarities exhibited by Gen. John Smith more closely fit Col. Johnson as does the timing of the work's release.[314]

> "A downright fire-eater, and no mistake. Showed that, I should say, to some purpose, in the late tremendous swamp-fight, away down South, with the Bugaboo and Kickapoo Indians." [Here my friend opened his eyes to some extent.] "Bless my soul!—blood and thunder, and all that!—prodigies of valor!—heard of him of course?—you know he's the man"
>
> "Smith!" said she in reply to my very earnest inquiry: "Smith!—why, not General John A. B. C.? Bless me, I thought you knew all about him! This is a wonderfully inventive age! Horrid affair that!—a bloody set of wretches, those Kickapoos!—fought like a hero— prodigies of valor— immortal renown. Smith!—Brevet Brigadier General John A. B. C.! Why, you know he's the man"[315]

Poe was also assaulting the Democratic Party's hero worship of such men as Andrew Jackson and Richard Mentor Johnson. They were hollow men who were the products of cults of personality. "I acknowledged his kindness in my best manner, and took leave of him at once, with a perfect understanding of the true state of affairs- with a full comprehension of the mystery which had troubled me so long. It was evident. It was a clear case. Brevet Brigadier General John A. B. C. Smith was the man—the man that was used up."[316] Paralleling the Whig campaign song of 1840, "Van, Van, Van is a used up man." Only a brief perusal of the various newspapers of the nation that year is necessary to turn up almost daily references to Johnson's war record and, "his *broken bones* and *mangled flesh*."[317] Legends sprang up of the still bleeding, almost stigmatic war wounds that he bore in penance for the nation.[318] The Star Spangled Banner was even reworked and used as a campaign song for Van Buren and Johnson.

> "Oh, say who is he through the forest so dark,
>
> With his warrior legions advancing to battle?
>
> Where the yell of the savage re-echoes- and hark!
>
> Where the death dealing strokes of their rifle balls rattle,
>
> What is it they fear?- 'tis the name that they hear,
>
> With the cry of revenge for the blood of the dear;
>
> 'Tis the name of our Johnson- oh, long will it flame,
>
> In letters of light on the banner of fame!"[319]

In a similar vein as Amos Kendall's letter to Van Buren about Johnson the tavern-keeper, a reporter for the *Cincinnati Evening Post* wrote an expose on both the Vice President's plantation and school in September 1839. The Colonel is painted in a similar light to the character of Kurtz in Conrad's *Heart of Darkness*, described as being clad in his morning gown regardless of the time of day and often being found living amongst the slave quarters. His "tavern" was little more than an overcrowded dining hall which served bad food, muddy water, and lacked ice. Worse yet, the famed academy so vaunted by both Johnson and the Democrats was home to dirty and half naked boys who, "looked around for a horse to watch, or any other such performance, to get a picayune, and convert it into grog– some of them were publically playing at cards to cheat each other of the earnings of the day." Finally on the night of the reporter's visit, the Vice President, still clad in his morning gown, led a concert and dance in which all races and classes mixed under the watchful eye of the Colonel.[320]

Harrison's campaign on the other hand was a masterpiece of electioneering. The Whigs managed to portray one of the wealthier men of the nation as a poor, log cabin, frontiersman in the best tradition of Andrew Jackson. This was served up as a foil to Van Buren's alleged elitism characterized by the golden spoons and carriages of Charles Ogle's famous "Gold Spoon Oration." The electioneering behind this motif involved posters, songs, souvenirs, marches, and the liberal distribution of alcohol to the masses in such a way to impress even the Democrats. Johnson himself recorded his disgust at the fact that, "I have seen ladies joining in the [Whigs] and wearing ribands across their breasts."[321] At the same time, Harrison's war record was trumpeted out to counter the one strength of Johnson. "Tippecanoe and Tyler Too" was served up to remind the voter that other people had defeated Tecumseh as well, in fact Harrison had accomplished that feat on multiple occasions. The Colonel's own words, spoken in support of his former commanding officer in front of Congress, were once again dredged up to damage him. "Of the career of General Harrison I need not speak- the history of the West, is his history. For forty years he has been identified with its interests, its perils, and its hopes ... During the late war, he was longer in active service than any other General Officer; he was perhaps oftener in action than any of them, and NEVER SUFFERED A DEFEAT."[322] For his own part, and in a credit to his nature as a loyal soldier, Johnson largely did nothing to retract these statements. In one particular case, the citizens of Greensburg, Pennsylvania wrote him on multiple occasions seeking for him to clarify his views on Harrison. The Vice President eventually responded stating that it was his, "custom not to give opinions upon mere matters of fact concerning public characters."[323] In many ways it was Johnson's own campaign in 1836 that had begun the road to the presidency for Harrison. The General had fallen on hard times following his retirement from the military, serving in a number of minor positions, being recalled as Minister to Colombia under a cloud of suspicion that he was sponsoring a coup, and was forced to supplant his meager income by distilling whiskey. Richard Johnson's resurrection of the Battle of the Thames necessarily brought renewed attention and fame to Gen. Harrison, fame that he would parlay into his candidacy in 1840.

During the last few months before the election Johnson was vigorously campaigning throughout the nation. The press followed him from speech to speech, celebratory dinner to celebratory dinner, and from rally to rally. His is reported to have delivered an oration at Bladensburg in Maryland while James Buchanan of Pennsylvania accompanied

Johnson on a speaking tour of New Jersey in July, during which time the two men stopped at Trenton and Princeton. Though Buchanan had been one of his ardent opponents during the convention, the two men now came together to defeat an even greater foe. Travelling westward he made several speeches in Columbus, Ohio where he was proclaimed the hero of the state and one of its greatest benefactors.[324] The next month he toured Harrisburg, Pennsylvania as well as New York City, dining with the city council at the American Hotel and meeting with local merchants and workers. Only a week later he was in Wheeling, Virginia seeking to gain support from those in the state who still supported him and his views. The end of August saw Johnson once again back in Ohio speaking at both Zanesville and Chillicothe, touting both his and Van Buren's 28 years of public service together as well as their combined unbounded support for the previous war. Finally, the Colonel turned southward and approached the Ohio River. At Franklin, between Dayton and Cincinnati, he was escorted into the town by thousands of citizens and soldiers in a procession reckoned to be over a mile in length. Once again he focused heavily on his accomplishment at the Thames rather than his legislative victories. After speaking before the Ohio Democratic Convention, Johnson traveled to the west and in September he was hosted by the Indiana Democratic State Central Committee at a dinner in his honor which was attended by some of the most important party members in the region. This was a state with a fair number of electoral votes in the old northwest which Van Buren was trailing in and would eventually lose by almost 10%.

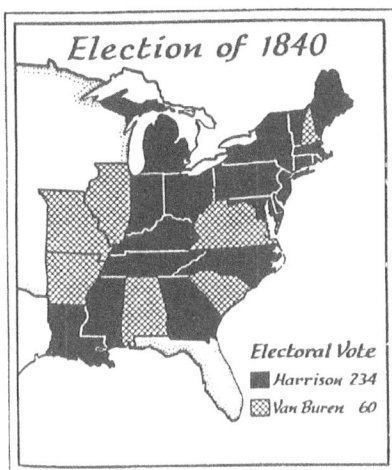

Image 13. The Election of 1840

Despite Johnson's best efforts, Van Buren was handily defeated receiving only 60 electoral votes to Harrison's 234. Johnson scored only 48 votes, with the remaining 12 going to Littleton Tazewell and James K. Polk. In a further humiliation, as the sitting officer of the Senate, he was required to read the election returns and announce his own replacement. Yet even Democratic papers complimented him for having, "pronounced his own defeat like a man; showing that the slayer of Tecumseh is not to be moved by trifles."[325] He was further applauded for the respect he paid to John Tyler during the transition period, while Van Buren was derided for stalking about the halls of the White House until the last possible hour before riding out early the next morning for New York, "avoiding the railroads and all public places."[326] Johnson even went so far as to dine with the incoming President shortly after the election. Ever the believer in patronage, he took the opportunity to ensure the continued service of his nephew Robert J. Ward who had been appointed a solicitor in the Land Office. Unfortunately though Harrison promised Johnson that his nephew would not be touched, he was quickly removed after the inauguration of the new administration.

Richard Mentor Johnson's time in the national spotlight was drawing to a close. If his vice presidency can be viewed as a failure it is largely due to his legacy being tied to Van Buren's disastrous presidency. As a testament to his accomplishment, however, it should be noted that only two Vice Presidents ever ran with their President for a second term during the nineteenth century. The first, Daniel D. Tompkins, ran with James Monroe in 1820 and both were unopposed by any other candidates, while the second was Richard Mentor Johnson in 1840. In fact another President–Vice President ticket would not run unchanged for a second term again until 1916. Though it is common since WWII for a President and Vice President to remain on the ticket for both terms, this was hardly the case during the first half of the nation's history. In the end, it wasn't Johnson's personal or professional life that cost the election for Van Buren. Rather the latter's own record over the previous four years, along with the successful electioneering of the Whigs, and voter fatigue with the Democratic party all contributed more so to Harrison's triumph.

CHAPTER VII

THE DAYS OF HEROES ARE OVER:
THE DECLINE OF RICHARD MENTOR JOHNSON

A bitter and disillusioned Johnson returned home from Washington DC to Kentucky in early 1841. Though he personally had been abandoned by his party, the Democrats themselves had been ousted by the entire nation. For the first time in 40 years, a non-Democrat sat in the White House. Likewise for the first time since Jefferson's Revolution of 1800, a non-Democratic majority held both houses of Congress. It would become a point of bitter contention between the different segments of the Democratic Party as to who and what was responsible for this tremendous loss, the failed policies, and poor appeal of Van Buren or the personal and political foibles of Johnson. Regardless, the stage seemed set for the adoption of the various Federalist/Whig policies and beliefs that Johnson had spent his life fighting against. Yet ever the committed warrior and still believing that it was his duty to aid the people, Johnson quickly set about attempting to reenter politics in his home state, with the hope of eventually returning to the national level. Yet with such a scandal filled background, a growing list of enemies, and an aging personal constitution, Johnson's prospects seemed slim. However, with his personal history of overcoming odds, the sexagenarian remained undaunted in the face of critics and pundits.

Despite some immediate reports that he had announced himself loyal to the Whig platform of Harrison, this was vehemently denied by both Johnson and his supporters. Johnson himself in a letter March 15, 1841, wrote, "If rumor can make my friends believe that I have changed or can change my position in politics it is very humiliating to me. The rumors of that kind cannot be worthy of anything but the lie direct from those who have confidence in me."[327] In fact by this point in his political career he had become associated with the Locofocos wing of the Democratic Party. Originating in New York in the mid-1830s, the group was originally named the Equal Rights Party but later adopted the sobriquet Locofocos after a popular brand of matches at the time.

According to party lore, the earliest adherents used the matches to light candles to carry on a political meeting after their Democratic rivals from Tammany Hall had shut off the flow of gas to the building. The Locofocos focused on issues confronting workers including free trade, more money in circulation, and labor unions. At the same time, they were decidedly opposed to any national or state bank as well as monopolies. They were the populist Democrats who would eventually seize control of the party by the turn of the century. Johnson's beliefs regarding the Bank and debtors prisons as well as his campaign on behalf of the common man fit in nicely with the philosophy of the group. Early on during the campaign of 1836, the Locofocos had thrown a dinner to honor Johnson, while refusing to acknowledge the presidential candidate that he was running with, Van Buren. Toasts were given against, "banks, banking, and paper money," issues perennially associated with Richard Mentor Johnson.[328] The Independent Treasury Bill, which was finally passed in 1840, was seen by the Locos to be a great victory for their cause and only further served to reinforce their faith in Johnson. The party even considered running him for President in 1844 as besides Van Buren he was the strongest natural choice and didn't have the stain of aristocracy often associated with Van Buren. A letter written that year described not only the Loco's desire to run Johnson but also his own hopes of gaining any position in order to get back into office. "If he can't get a White wife, he is content to live with a colored one, and when he sells her, or she dies—why he just takes one of the 'Ebon maids' again (ergo) If he can't get the presidency he will take the vice presidents place again."[329]

EFFECT OF THE HARD CIDER PRESS ON LOCO FOCO PIPPINS

Image 14. Johnson and the Locofocos

From 1841 to 1843, Johnson was again in the Kentucky state legislature, having been elected without opposition only three months after his return from the capital. Yet he continued to spend a majority of his time running his plantation and tending bar at his tavern. Financial difficulties continued to plague the once wealthy and powerful politician as did a certain sense of malaise towards his current position. Not content to fade away at the state level, Johnson challenged Crittenden for his Senate seat in 1842. Yet Whiggery was sweeping both the state and the nation after almost 40 years of Democratic rule and he was soundly defeated. However, it appears from several contemporary letters that he did not seriously consider the position. Governor Robert P. Letcher wrote to Crittenden that, "Col. Richard Johnson is now with me; he will act the gentleman, and go for you 'through thick and thin.' Had a long talk with him since I commenced this letter. He will carry with him as many friends as he can, and really I must tell you that you are not to forget his honorable feelings and fair dealing. I know you like him, and you ought to like him."[330] While the following day he penned that, "Colonel Johnson has just left me again, after *renewing his bond of fidelity*. We are getting very thick, I can tell you. If I had time I would make you laugh heartily about many matters connected with this election. Oh, the duplicity of this world."[331] From a subsequent correspondence, it appears that the old Vice President played his part well during the election in the Kentucky legislature, telling Gov. Letcher that, "he had never exerted himself so much in all his life to keep down a damned factious opposition of damned rascally Whigs, as well as Democrats."[332] In fact Johnson was reentering politics in Kentucky at a particularly poor time for his party. The Whig Party would monopolize the Senate seats from the state and most of the House of Representative ones as well until almost the start of the Civil War. He may have hoped that by supporting the local establishment he would perhaps be able to rise locally, or at least be treated better than by this own party which had all but excluded him.

The other famous War Hawk from Kentucky, Henry Clay, had already removed himself from the Senate in 1840 to prepare for a run for President in 1844. Johnson hoped to challenge his fellow Kentuckian, but first need to once again gain the support of Democrats. Yet most of the leaders of the party had now fully lost confidence in his abilities and health. As early as 1842 in a letter to Sen. John Crittenden, Gov. Robert Perkins Letcher wrote that, "Johnson ... seems to understand very well Mr. V Buren is stacking the cards, but he will have to stand it. Dick is much the best fellow of the two; but he will be *bamboozled* as sure as a gun. He intimated to me he would prefer Clay next to himself to any man in the Union. You never saw a more restless dissatisfied man in your life, than Dick."[333] While William Marcy opined that, "he is not now even what he formally was. It may be there was never so much of him as many of us were led to suppose." Calhoun confided to a friend that, "his [Johnson] case is hopeless ... the days of heroes are over," while elsewhere referring to him as, "a mass of stupidity, vulgarity, and immorality."[334] Even his old ally Jackson confessed to Van Buren that Johnson would be little more than a drag on the national ticket.[335] This despite Johnson's wintering with Jackson at the Hermitage in the winter of 1841–1842. Crittenden as well, shortly after his win over Johnson for the Senate seat in January 1842, expressed shock that, "Johnson has allowed himself to be drawn into the commission of a sad error ... as a candidate for the Presidency, he ought not have exposed himself to such a defeat." He went on to surmise that the Colonel may have been tricked into running for the Senate by his less than loyal friends in the Democratic Party who did, "so for the purpose of killing him off out of Van Buren's Way."[336] If so, it was a career ending maneuver.

Yet all of this did not stop Johnson from actively seeking a presidential or vice presidential nomination. As early as January 1842, the *New York* Tribune was reporting that the Democrats in Kentucky were proposing to run him for President.[337] That same month he gave a rousing speech to the Friends of Ireland in Frankfort while a year later he met with the United Irish Repeal Association in New York. The Black Forties were just beginning to take hold on the Emerald Isle, and the Irish were quickly becoming an important component of the northern Democratic Party, particularly its Locofocs faction. In fact Johnson compared the moral struggle of the Irish against the British Empire to his own party's efforts against the dominant power of, "the eastern sun."[338] Previously in the 1840 election, an Ohio newspaper urged local Irish immigrants to turn out and support Van Buren and Johnson against the, "British Whiggery," of Harrison.[339] A convention held in the state of Mississippi in 1842 once again nominated both Van Buren and Johnson for the presidency and vice presidency, though the latter's name was then struck off the ticket and replaced by James K. Polk.[340] Johnson also famously toured the state of Illinois in May 1843, where he was touted by Gov. John Reynolds who as early as 1841 had called the Kentuckian, "the friend of the West, and the Advocate of the reduction of the price of public lands."[341] For three days he visited Belleville, Jacksonville, and Springfield meeting supporters and giving speeches. The reception in Springfield was described days later by the *Illinois State Register* as, "an event which will occur but once in a lifetime."[342] Sitting in a carriage pulled by four horses and preceded by various military and musical bands, Johnson arrived at the Illinois State House to a cheering throng of people. After a rousing welcome by the Secretary of State filled with classical allusions, Johnson ascended to the speaker's platform and delivered a two-hour address. Yet once again the decline of the man was evident. Though supporters at the time praised its, "patriotic eloquence," their additional reference to it lacking, "the slightest preparation," though meant to convey a sense of wonder, instead delivers a blunt truism.[343] Instead of a rousing speech given by a man who knew this was his last chance at office, Johnson instead fell back on his tale of bravery at the Thames. Later that night he attended a dinner thrown in his honor where he reaffirmed his commitment to the acquisition of Oregon by any means and that Sunday Johnson attended both a Methodist as well as Baptist service. By late 1842, the former Vice President even felt confident enough to assure Gov. Letcher of Kentucky that he would take Pennsylvania from Buchanan.[344]

Image 15. Johnson by John Neagle (1843)

However, as the national convention grew closer, it was becoming painfully obvious to Johnson that his chances were slim. "Dick Johnson ... begins to think the Locofoco leaders will shuffle him out of the contest ... he will gladly take the Vice Presidency."[345] Still a loyal contingent of his supporters dutifully gathered at the Democratic convention in Baltimore in 1844, described by Calhoun as, "an abortion," of a meeting, to push for the former Vice President.[346] When his name was brought up for discussion they waved his signature scarlet vest and cheered and hooted for five straight minutes.[347] Van Buren's inability to gather the necessary two-thirds vote due to an emerging north–south split in the party over the issue of the annexation of Texas meant that the floor was wide open for a nomination, giving hope to Johnson and his followers. On the first ballot Van Buren polled 146 delegates, Lewis Cass 83, and Johnson 24. On subsequent ballots Van Buren began a decline that would see him drop ultimately to 100 while Cass and Johnson continued to rise. The Kentuckian though would top out at 38 votes and by the eighth ballot had given up. His personal history was again brought up by southern Democrats along with an imagined alliance between him and Clay stretching back 40 years in an effort to further sabotage his chances. In the end, a fellow westerner and a dark horse, James K. Polk of Tennessee, clinched the nomination. Though unknown to many Americans, Polk was well acquainted with Johnson, as he had been put forward by Jackson as a possible replacement for the Colonel in 1840. Johnson's people still hoped for a spot as Polk's running mate, but received only a paltry 26 of the 266 votes available during deliberation, with only Pennsylvania supporting him. Though several small, loyal state conventions arose afterwards in order to push the candidacy of Johnson, most notably at Buffalo, his pledge to support the national ticket soon led to their dissolution.

Though Johnson was not an active member of the Election of 1844 he did become passively involved. Whig newspapers vied with each other to find decades old speeches by Col. Johnson in order to find some small approving phrase about Henry Clay. Likewise the Whig candidate frequently compared himself in speeches and letters to Van Buren and Johnson, using them as a foil to his character and ideas. This was necessitated in part by the dark horse status of Polk. Several Democratic newspapers did run letters from Johnson expressing his support for Polk, but these short, formal, and lacked any of the fire with which the man had defended Van Buren, Jackson, Jefferson, or even Harrison. Yet Polk's promises of territorial expansion and lower tariffs combined with Clay's ambiguous positions on Texas and recollections of the Corrupt Bargain of 1825 to ensure a southern Democratic victory.

For his part Richard Mentor Johnson was in favor of the annexation of Texas. This view was in keeping with many of his past actions and views. In a letter on the subject written in the spring of 1844 in response to an inquiry from a political committee in Pittsburgh, Johnson took the stance that Texas had always been a part of Louisiana. "The first public act of my life was the raising of a company of volunteers to descend our western waters to New Orleans upwards of forty years ago to vindicate our right," a move he repeated the next decade and one he was willing to do again against Mexico. As to the question of slavery, the Colonel's response reiterated his previous support for the people of Missouri to decide the issue for themselves as well as his views on the ability of individuals to decide matters of theology expressed in the Sunday Mail Reports. He finished out his letter with a telling view on the situation that was to arise in the nation less than a generation later. "Our country is an identity, and cannot be divided without ruin."[348] In fact many in Texas thought Johnson to be one of their strongest allies. In a letter to Sam Houston written in May 1844, James Pinckney Henderson, the former Texan ambassador to France and Secretary of States, expressed his opinion that, "the whole country is becoming aroused on the subject of annexation and should the Democratic Convention at Baltimore on Monday unite upon Genl Cass and Coln Johnson, Clay will easily be defeated."[349]

The last six years of Johnson's life were a mixture of depression and failure, a slow descent into obscurity interrupted by brief moments of promise. He was honored in October 1845 by being named one of the pallbearers for the re-internment of Daniel Boone's remains. The removal of the body from Missouri to Kentucky in July of that year, headed by his old nemesis Thomas Crittenden, caused quite a controversy at the time and since, as many in his family and the state did not wish him moved. Some have claimed that the very identity of his remains was questionable or that not all of the bones were disinterred.[350] The grave of the legendary Kentuckian would end up being quite near to the final resting place of Johnson himself.

These years also witnessed the outbreak of the Mexican War and the continuance of Manifest Destiny. Johnson, ever the patriot, even volunteered to serve in the Army once that conflict erupted, but his offer was rejected by Polk. Instead he helped to recruit other soldiers from his home state as he had back in 1812. Only a week after the official declaration of war between the two nations, Johnson was in Baltimore delivering an address to hundreds of volunteers. He did though warn the nation against celebrating the accomplishments of the early part of the war too prematurely. Knowing full well how deadly wars could become, he cautioned that these first victories were but, "a wedding and dinner party," compared to what could come.[351] Likewise during the war scare of 1845 that arose during the Oregon Country dispute, Johnson responded to a question about his willingness to once again engage his old foe. "I stopped five bullets and my mare fifteen in the last war, and I think I am good for one yet."[352] At the same time his name surfaced as a possible candidate to be the first governor of the new territory of Oregon, though this also amounted to nothing once a bill proposed by Senator Brown endorsing this was voted down in Congress in 1845.[353] As a local paper lamented, "The Hero of the Thames is just the man to lead such an enterprise, and lay the foundation of a Republican State on the Pacific."[354] He was however appointed by President Taylor in September 1849 to serve as secretary to the Mexican commissioners to investigate unresolved land claims in California left over from the war.[355]

He nevertheless continued to fight for the causes of the poor and oppressed, beseeching Congress for more funds for schools for Indians as well as becoming active in movements to ban capital punishment within the nation. On religious as well as practical grounds, he considered the practice to be unjust and ineffective as, "the object of human laws is not to mete out strict justice without mercy."[356] So vigorous was some of his work that observers at the time posited that, "since his retirement from public life, his health is entirely restored, his constitution reinvigorated, and that his intellect is much brighter than it was a few years ago."[357]

Johnson tried twice in 1848 to once again run for office but lost both elections. The first was yet another contest against Henry Clay for a Senate seat. Unfortunately, as both houses of the Kentucky legislature were in Whig hands, Clay's win like that of Crittenden before him was almost preordained. Johnson received only 45 votes in the election while Clay scored an impressive 92. At the same time, larger forces were at work as some Whigs were eager to possibly run Clay for President in 1852 and expanded much influence to ensure a strong election for him. The second campaign involved Johnson running for Governor of Kentucky as an independent candidate. In the latter instance, he ultimately withdrew so as not to harm the chance of Democratic candidate Lazarus W. Powell after a personal meeting with the candidate. In the end, despite Johnson then actively campaigning for Powell the Whig Crittenden still managed to win Kentucky, showing the declining power and influence of Johnson in even his home state. Though with his pervious support of Crittenden only a few years before, Johnson's overall motives remain suspect.

Likewise his proposals to Congress, especially for renewed funding for his school for Indian children, began to fall upon deaf ears as even fellow Democrats, such as William D. Sawyer of Ohio, began to question his alleged fraud and corruption.[358] The school had been moved to Oklahoma in 1843 largely under the suggestion of Peter Pitchlynn as he felt it would be more effective to be nearer to the various reservations. The ill will between Johnson and Pitchlynn had never subsided since the latter's expose back in 1828. We find Johnson writing to Secretary of War John Spencer in 1841 complaining that Pitchlynn had assisted in the flight of a dozen students, "Pitchlynn has determined to destroy the school."[359] An amendment to the Indian appropriations bill for 1848 granting Johnson $10,000 for a new school was quietly laid aside as concerns over both him and the concept mounted.

The Election of 1848 in fact largely passed without the presence of Richard Mentor Johnson, a man who had been heavily involved in almost every convention and contest since 1804. His shadow though still hovered over the election. Lewis Cass, the Democratic nominee, had been present with Johnson during the charge at the Thames, fighting with James Johnson against the British on the right. Yet Van Buren's entrance into the conflict as the Free Soil candidate managed to steal enough votes, especially in New York, to ensure a Whig victory much as the Liberty Party had helped to propel Polk into the White House in 1844. Johnson's last political action in the capital was his appearance at the inauguration of Zachary Taylor where he sat next to outgoing Vice President George M. Dallas, the hero of one war watching the rise to power of the hero of another.[360]

The last year of Johnson's life was spent in declining health, with him suffering from a number of "paralytic attacks." The *Louisville Daily Journal* described him in 1850 as, "laboring under an attack of dementia, which renders him totally unfit for business. It is painful to see him on the floor attempting to discharge the duties of a member. He is incapable of properly exercising his physical or mental powers."[361] He spent the majority of his time on his farm with a handful of elderly and infirm slaves, several mulattos, and Patience Chinn, having transferred the rest of his slave holdings to his surviving daughter. Despite this, he continued to involve himself in the affairs of the nation, penning a letter in June 1850 approving of what would eventually become the Compromise of 1850. Johnson explained that while we would always have political parties who differed as to ideas and methods, the maintenance of the union was a core principle for both Whigs and Democrats. As to the issue of slavery, "southern rights must be respected—the Constitution must be sustained, and the Federal Union must be preserved." The former President of the Senate ended his letter explaining that the vitriol and potential disaster which was accompanying this debate was exactly why he never allowed an abolitionist proposal to be submitted to Congress during his tenure.[362]

Johnson also openly discussed once again running for governor of the state.[363] Following the departure of the popular Whig legislator Howard Smith, who Johnson had vowed not to run against, the aged Vice President's prospects suddenly improved.[364] Though he was elected to the state legislature in August 1850, he was unable to take his seat, for on November 19, 1850, at 9:00 in the morning Richard Mentor Johnson suffered a fatal stroke and died. Flags in all Democratic cities were lowered to half-mast while politicians in New York wore badges of mourning for 30 days and its Democratic organization held a memorial service.[365] Even abolitionists celebrated his conduct towards his mixed race children, praising it as the example to strive for in the nation.[366]

During the memorial at Tammany Hall in early December, a eulogy was offered up by John C. Mather, a prominent Democrat who would later go on to become the first official ever impeached in the state of New York. The fine paean, perhaps better than anything else, sums up his life and meaning to his contemporaries.

> "Richard Mentor Johnson, the hero, the patriot, the statesman is no more ... Of the last moments of the illustrious dead, we have few particulars. But we know that he died, as for the last forty years he lived, *with his armor on* ... His history is interwoven with that of his country for the last half century ... It is impossible to say whether Col. Johnson wielded his pen or his sword with the most vigor and efficiency. With the one he did good service for his country on the frontier, with the other he achieved a moral victory over fanaticism and religious bigotry ... the distinguishing trait of his political character was its *nationality* ... he preferred the prosperity and the happiness of all to any temporary advantage he might gain as the leader of a new sectional party."[367]

The funeral of Richard Mentor Johnson was worthy of a Roman consul or fallen hero. The city of Frankfort ground to a halt as the coffin of the former Vice President was carried at noon to the legislative building. Draped in flags that had been carried by Kentucky soldiers during the Mexican War, including at Buena Vista, it was borne in a procession of politicians, mourners, soldiers, judges, and citizens. Slowly it moved through the capital and was brought to rest at the Frankfort Cemetery. Guns were shot off in salute as the great Kentucky lawgiver was laid to rest, soon to be followed less than two years later by his former friend and now political foil Henry Clay.[368]

The hero of the Thames and former Vice President was laid to rest at Frankfort Cemetery in Frankfort, Kentucky. His monument, designed by Robert E. Launitz and erected by the commonwealth in 1852 for the cost of $2,400, only $900 of which was provided for by the state, was placed close to the state's monument to its wartime dead erected after the Mexican War. According to one traveler to the state in 1855, "the design is a broken column placed on a shaft, and the fracture draped with a blanket, on which stands an eagle with a civic wreath; on the base are sculptured a large medallion bust, and a bas relief of his conflict with Tecumseh."[369] On its front stands the following inscription summing up the accomplishments of the man ...

"To The Memory Of
Colonel Richard M. Johnson
A Faithful Public Servant
For Nearly Half A Century As A Member
Of The Kentucky Legislature And
Representative And Senator In Congress:
Author Of The Sunday Mail Report
And Of The Laws Abolishing Imprisonment
For Debt In Kentucky
And In The United States;
Distinguished By His Valour
As Colonel Of A Kentucky Regiment
In The Battle Of The Thames;
For Four Years Vice-President
Of The United States.
Kentucky, His Native State
To Mark The Sense Of His Eminent Service
In The Cabinet And In The Field
Has Erected This Monument
In The Resting Place Of
Her Illustrious Dead."

Honors trickled in for years afterwards with the states of Illinois, Iowa, Kentucky, Missouri, and Nebraska all naming counties after him. In 1895 his bust, designed by James Paxton Voorhees, was placed in the Senate after the passing of a resolution calling for a gallery of vice presidential statues. Yet his memory quickly faded from the national consciousness. His family as well largely subsided into obscurity. Courts ruled that due to the illegitimacy of his remaining daughter, she could not inherit her father's property. Instead it was split among two of his surviving brothers and various other family members. It is doubtful that many of his descendants today even know of the blood that runs in their veins from Richard Mentor Johnson and Julia Chinn. His memory has been stricken from the nation in the best tradition of the ancient practice of *damnatio memoriae*.

Image 16. The Grave of Richard Mentor Johnson

The New Jersey newspaper, the *Trenton Emporium*, once opined, "what hand, when he dies, will be worthy to write his epitaph?"[370] Few authors or historians have tried over the past century to answer this challenge, with no major biography of him being written since the campaign literature of the 1830s. Hopefully, the above attempt once again exposes the nation to one of its more colorful, heroic, and eccentric characters. Richard Mentor Johnson's life stands out as both uniquely nineteenth century as well as surprisingly modern. His unabashed logrolling and quasi-ethical patronage practices fit well in either century while his personal relationship could be exaggerated to be a proud stance on untraditional marriage. Perhaps an Ohio newspaperman writing during the 1840 campaign season best summed up the man, "in Richard M. Johnson we find the Patriot, the Statesman, the Warrior, and the Veteran, so happily combined and blended together, as to form the whole souled man."[371] His life and accomplishments impacted not only himself, or his own state, but the entire nation as well. The final scene in

Richard Emmons' partisan political play about Johnson best displayed this idea. As the wounded and bleeding Colonel lay unconscious on the stage floor, the entire cast gathered over him, proclaiming Johnson to be, "the Champion of his Country."[372]

Postscript
The Sins of the Father

The death of Richard Mentor Johnson was a loss for not only the nation and Democratic Party, but for the Johnson family as well. His children, including those he recognized as well as his other illegitimate offspring, would not continue the celestially bound upward trend of the family which was established with William Johnson in Virginia and continued with both Robert and Richard in Kentucky. Racism, political differences, civil war, hard economic times, and poor luck soon brought the once promising family to earth.

His eldest daughter, Adaline, had died around 1836 possibly in childbirth or from complications arising from it, leaving behind only one child. Her son, Robert Johnson Scott, was raised by his father who remarried but continued to live within Scott County in Kentucky. He was sent to Shurtleff College in Illinois, the oldest Baptist school west of the Appalachian Mountains, where he completed his education before returning to the family farm. With the approach of the Civil War, the family divested themselves of slaves while Robert himself married in the late 1850s and settled on a farm in Buena Vista, Illinois not far from the Mississippi River. Here, he continued his studies, eventually becoming a physician. Much like his grandfather, Robert Johnson Scott lost the majority of his fortune to a series of poor investments and was left poverty stricken. He moved his family to Brookfield, Missouri a year after the ending of the Civil War with only, "two teams and one hundred and twenty-five dollars in money."[373] Elizabeth Johnson divorced Robert two years later in 1868 as his fortunes fell further. Yet the genetic predisposition of the Johnsons to rise in the face of adversity led Robert to not only turn his fortunes around by investing in a local railroad line, but also to remarry and develop a successful medical practice. Four children resulted from his marriages, Edward Bion Scott (b.1859), Thomas Frederic Scott (b.1861), Frances Scott (b.1863), and Ira Mentor Scott (b.1871). Robert remained a prominent member of the community until his death in 1905.

Of his children, Ira Mentor Scott became a plumber working with the city water department and dying childless in Brookfield a day before the death of his second wife in January 1944. Robert's first born son, Edward Bion Scott, moved with his mother to Los Angeles, California some time before the turn of the century. Here, he worked as a printer and married Lulla Rebecca Dorn, a marriage that would also produce no children. Thomas Frederic Scott returned to Illinois, living in Cass County and working as a carpenter. He would go on to have two surviving sons, Thomas Payne (b.1894) who relocated to Berkeley, California and Robert Frederic (b.1899). Overall, the Johnson family descended from Adaline steadily declined in its socioeconomic status as the years wore on and it scattered across the west, with most branches dying off entirely.

Imogene Johnson Pence would continue to reside in Kentucky with her husband until her death in 1883. As mentioned previously, the Kentucky courts were quick to divest Richard Mentor Johnson's property following his demise, leaving Imogene and her husband in financial constraint. Their marriage would ultimately produce six surviving children, Richard Mentor Johnson Pence (b.1831), Amanda Malvina Pence (b.1833), Mary Jane Pence (b.1835), Daniel Franklin Pence (b. 1850), Albert Pence (b.1852), and Edward Herndon Pence (b.1858). Of these, Richard and Albert would die after only a few years while Edward would produce no known heirs, further reducing the size of the family. The three remaining siblings would go on to have around 15 children.

Mary Jane Pence married her cousin Josiah Pence in 1851 and the two continued to reside in Scott County, Kentucky until their respective deaths. Census records from the time show them to have had four children, William Henry (b.1852), Anna (b.1857), Daniel (b.1863), and Emma (b.1868). These records also list a number of black servants as living in the household or next door headed by a George Johnson who was born around 1845. While it was not uncommon for freed slaves to adopt the surname of their former masters, the paternity of George is questionable.

William H. Pence married Cora Offutt around 1885 and a few years later moved his family to Cincinnati, Ohio. Here, he worked as a miller and had three sons, Robert (b.1886), Joseph (b.1888), and Leroy (b.1906). By 1920, this portion of the Pence family had once again relocated, this time to Flint, Michigan where William and his wife would remain until their deaths. Daniel Pence married Leila Hart in 1887 and likewise moved north to Ohio in the early 1900s. He would work as a furniture maker in a series of factories and eventually had two surviving children, Bessie Mary (b.1888) and Edna E. (b.1890). The former would marry William Bolland but have no recorded children while the latter would never marry and died in Baton Rouge in 1981. Anna Mary J. Pence remained within the area of Scott County, Kentucky, marrying James L. Jackson in 1875. The marriage would produce one son, William Claude Jackson (b.1880) who worked as a realtor in Lexington for years and at the time of his death in 1970 was survived by four grandchildren and three great grandchildren. Finally, Emma Pence likewise spent her life in Kentucky, marrying John Duncan a local salesman and having six children.

Amanda Malvina Pence married Robert M. Lee in 1846 and the two would reside in Scott County until their deaths. At least four children were born to the couple, Mary Lee (b.1851), Ada Lee (b.1859), Robert E. Lee (b.1863), and Daniel Franklin Lee (b.1875). The naming of their second child clearly expresses a certain level of sympathy for the southern cause then raging at the time. Ada and Daniel would die relatively young while Robert would never marry. Mary would marry Virgil W. Easley and have four surviving children, Lutie Cecilia Easley (b.1874), Edward Pence Easley (b.1876), Mallie J. Easley (b.1879), and Ella Easley (b.1884).

The final child of Imogene Johnson was Daniel Pence. He, like most of his other siblings and relatives, would spend the entirety of his life within Kentucky as a small farmer. After marrying Ella D. Smith in 1883, the couple had four children, Gracie Maria Pence (b.1884), William Collis Pence (b.1885), Edward Herndon Pence (b.1888), and Laura Imogene Pence (b.1895). The descendants of Daniel Pence proved to be the largest driving force behind the continuation of the Johnson line with numerous descendants populating the region for the next century.

The various alleged offspring of the Vice President will be left out of this genealogical study. Evidence to their true paternity remains lacking and as such speculation should be avoided. It is sufficient enough to say that the possibility exists that numerous other modern day Americans may be descended from Johnson through various branches that will remain perhaps forever unknown.

Overall, the Johnson dynasty which began in Virginia and was thereafter transplanted to Kentucky dwindled almost immediately after the death of Vice President Richard Mentor Johnson. While his siblings and their progeny would go on to have somewhat illustrious careers, this was not to be the case for the children of Richard's two daughters. Certainly, the racial makeup of his children was the primary cause of this, though Johnson's own financial constraints surely also handicapped his immediate descendants. The majority of those living today who are related to him are probably unaware of the blood that flows through their veins. Yet though Richard Mentor Johnson may not have passed on a sizeable inheritance to his kin, his indomitable spirit and indefatigable courage hopefully disseminated down the generations. Even if he had given nothing to his descendants, his accomplishments while alive more than benefited the entirety of the American population. Despite his personal foibles, character flaws, and occasional corruption, his mark on American history overall should be recorded as a positive one.

APPENDIX I

Sunday Mail Report (1829)

The Committee, to whom were referred the several petitions on the subject of Mails on the Sabbath, or the first day of the week, report—

That some respite is required from the ordinary vocations of life, is an established principle, sanctioned by the usages of all nations, whether Christian or Pagan. One day in seven has also been determined upon as the proportion of time; and in conformity with the wishes of the great majority of citizens of this country, the first day of the week, commonly called Sunday, has been set apart to that object. The principle has received the sanction of the national legislature, so far as to admit a suspension of all public business on that day, except in cases of absolute necessity, or of great public utility. This principle the committee would not wish to disturb. If kept within its legitimate sphere of action, no injury can result from its observance. It should, however, be kept in mind, that the proper object of government is to protect all persons in the enjoyment of their religious as well as civil rights, and not to determine for any whether they shall esteem one day above another, or esteem all days alike holy.

We are aware that a variety of sentiment exists among the good citizens of this nation on the subject of the Sabbath day; and our government is designed for the protection of one as much as for another.

The Jews, who in this country are as free as Christians, and entitled to the same protection from the laws, derive their obligation to keep the Sabbath day from the fourth commandment of their decalogue, and in conformity with that injunction, pay religious homage to the seventh day of the week, which we call Saturday. One denomination of Christians among us, justly celebrated for their piety, and certainly as good Christians as any other class, agree with the Jews in the moral obligation of the Sabbath, and observe the same day; there are, also, many Christians among us who derive their obligation to observe the Sabbath from the decalogue, but regard the Jewish Sabbath as abrogated. From the example of the Apostles of Christ, they have chosen the first day of the week, instead of that day set apart in the decalogue, for their religious devotions. They have generally regarded the observance of the day as a devotional exercise, and would not more readily enforce it on others than they would enforce secret prayer or meditation.

Urging the fact that neither the Lord nor his disciples, though often censured by their accusers for a violation of the Sabbath, ever enjoined its observance, they regarded it as a subject on which every person should be fully persuaded in his own mind, and not coerce others to act upon his persuasion. Many Christians again differ from these, professing to derive their obligation to observe the Sabbath from the fourth commandment of the Jewish decalogue, and bring the example of the Apostles, who appear to have held their public meetings for worship on the first day of the week, as authority for so far changing the decalogue as to substitute that day for the seventh.

The Jewish government was a theocracy, which enforced religious observances; and though the committee would hope that no portion of the citizens of our country would willingly introduce a system of religious coercion in our civil institutions, the example of other nations should admonish us to watch carefully against its earliest indication. With these different views the committee are of opinion that Congress cannot interfere. It is not the legitimate province of the legislature to determine what religion is true or what false. Our government is a civil, and not a religious institution. Our constitution recognises in every person the right to choose his own religion, and to enjoy it freely without molestation. Whatever may be the religious sentiments of citizens, and however variant, they are alike entitled to protection from the government, so long as they do not invade the rights of others.

The transportation of the mail on the first day of the week, it is believed, does not interfere with the rights of conscience. The petitioners for its discontinuance appear to be actuated from a religious zeal, which may be commendable if confined to its proper sphere; but they assume a position better suited to an ecclesiastical than a civil institution. They appear in many instances to lay it down as an axiom that the practice is a violation of the law of God. Should Congress, in their legislative capacity, adopt that sentiment, it would establish the principle that the legislature is a proper tribunal to determine what are the laws of God. It would involve a legislative decision in a religious controversy; and in a point in which good citizens may honestly differ in opinion without disturbing the peace of society, or endangering its liberties. If this principle is once introduced, it will be impossible to define its bounds. Among all the religious persecutions with which almost every page of modern history is stained, no victim ever suffered but for the violation of what government denominated the law of God. To prevent a similar train of evils in this country, the constitution has wisely withheld from our government the power of defending the divine law. It is a right reserved for each citizen; and while he respects the equal rights of others he cannot be held amenable to any human tribunal for his conclusions.

Extensive religious combinations to effect a political

object are, in the opinion of the committee, always dangerous. The first effort of the kind calls for the establishment of a principle which, in the opinion of the committee, would lay the foundation for dangerous innovation upon the spirit of the constitution and upon the religious rights of the citizens. If admitted, it may be justly apprehended that the future measures of government will be strongly marked, if not eventually controlled, by the same influence. All religious despotism commences by combination and influence, and when that influence begins to operate upon the political institutions of our country, the civil power soon bends under it, and the catastrophe of other nations furnishes an awful warning of the consequence.

Under the present regulations of the post office department, the rights of conscience are not invaded. Every agent enters voluntarily, and it is presumed conscientiously, into the discharge of his duties, without intermeddling with the conscience of another. Post offices are so regulated as that but a small proportion of the first day of the week is required to be occupied in official business. In the transportation of the mail on that day no one agent is employed many hours. Religious persons enter into the business without violating their own consciences, or imposing any restraints upon others. Passengers in the mail stages are free to rest during the first day of the week, or to pursue their journeys at their own pleasure. While the mail is transported on Saturday, the Jew and the Sabbatarian may abstain from any agency in carrying it, from conscientious scruples. While it is transported on the first day of the week, another class may abstain from the same religious scruples. The obligation of government is the same to both of these classes, and the committee can discover no principle on which the claims of one should be more respected than those of the other, unless it should be admitted that the consciences of the minority are less sacred than those of the majority.

It is the opinion of the committee that the subject should be regarded simply as a question of expediency, irrespective of its religious bearing. In this light it has hitherto been considered. Congress has never legislated upon the subject. It rests, as it has ever done, in the legal discretion of the postmaster-general, under the repeated refusal of Congress to discontinue the Sabbath mails. His knowledge and judgment in all the concerns of that department will not be questioned. His intense labours and assiduity have resulted in the highest improvement of every branch of his department. It is practised only on the great leading mail routes, and such others as are necessary to maintain their connexions. To prevent this, would in the opinion of the committee, be productive of immense injury, both in its commercial, political, and in its moral bearings.

The various departments of government require frequently in peace, always in war, the speediest intercourse with the remotest parts of the country; and one important object of the mail establishment is to furnish the greatest and most economical facilities for such intercourse. The delay of the mails one day in seven would require the employment of special expresses at great expense, and sometimes with great uncertainty. The commercial, manufacturing, and agricultural interests of our country are so intimately connected as to require a constant and the most expeditious correspondence betwixt all our seaports, and betwixt them and the most interior settlements. The delay of mails during Sunday would give occasion to the employment of private expresses to such an amount that probably ten riders would be employed where one mail stage is now running on that day; thus diverting the revenue of that department into another channel, and sinking the establishment into a state of pusillanimity incompatible with the dignity of the government of which it is a department.

Passengers in the mail stages, if the mails are not permitted to proceed on Sunday, will be expected to spend that day at a tavern upon the road, generally under circumstances not friendly to devotion, and at an expense which many are but poorly able to encounter. To obviate these difficulties many will employ extra carriages for their conveyance, and become the bearers of correspondence, as more expeditious than the mail. The stage proprietors will themselves often furnish the travellers with these means of conveyance, so that the effect will ultimately be only to stop the mail, while the vehicle which conveys it will continue, and its passengers become the special messengers for conveying a considerable portion of what would otherwise constitute the contents of the mail. Nor can the committee discover when the system could consistently end.

If the observance or a holy day become incorporated in our institutions, shall we not forbid the movement of an army, prohibit an assault in time of war, and lay an injunction upon our naval officers to lie in the wind while upon the ocean on that day? Consistency would seem to require it. Nor is it certain that we should stop here. If the principle is once established that religion or religious observances shall be interwoven with our legislative acts, we must pursue it to its ultimatum.

We shall, if consistent, provide for the erection of edifices for the worship of the Creator, and for the support of Christian ministers, if we believe such measures will promote the interests of Christianity. It is the settled conviction or the committee that the only method of avoiding these consequences, with their attendant train of evils, is to adhere strictly to the spirit of the constitution, which regards the general government in no other light than that of a civil institution, wholly destitute of religious authority.

What other nations call religious toleration we call religious rights. They are not exercised in virtue of governmental indulgence, but as rights, of which government cannot deprive any portion of citizens, however small. Despotic power may invade those rights, but justice still confirms them. Let the national legislature once perform an act which involves the decision of a religious controversy, and it will have passed its legitimate bounds. The precedent will then be established, and the foundation laid for that usurpation of the Divine prerogative in this country, which has been the desolating scourge to the fairest portions of the world.

Our constitution recognises no other power than that of persuasion for enforcing religious observances. Let the professors of Christianity recommend their religion by deeds of benevolence—by Christian meekness—by love of temperance and holiness. Let them combine their efforts to instruct the ignorant, to relieve the widow and the orphan, to promulgate to the world the gospel of their Saviour, recommending its precepts by their habitual example; government will find its legitimate object in protecting them. It cannot oppose them, and they will not need its aid. Their moral influence will then do infinitely more to advance the true interests of religion than any measures they may call on Congress to enact.

The petitioners do not complain of any infringement upon their own rights. They enjoy all that Christians ought to ask at the hand of any government—protection from all molestation in the exercise of their religious sentiments.

Resolved, That the committee be discharged from the further consideration of the subject.

APPENDIX II

GENEALOGIES

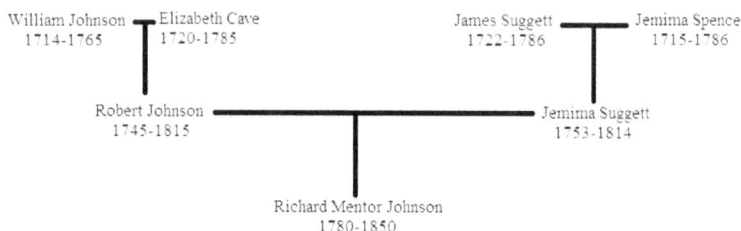

Figure 1. Immediate Ancestry of Richard M. Johnson

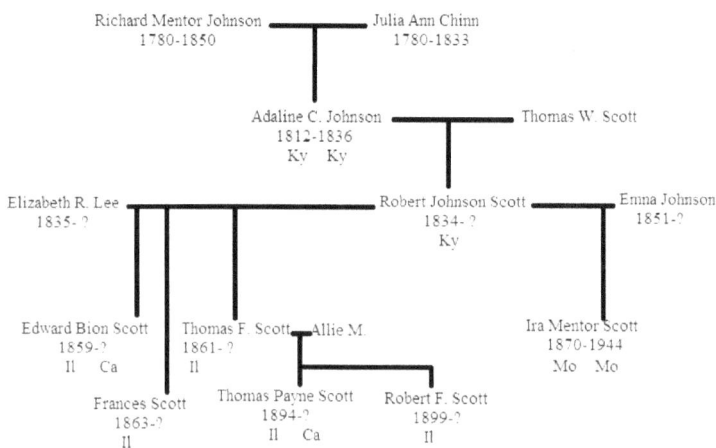

Figure 2. Descendants of Richard M. Johnson Through Adaline Johnson

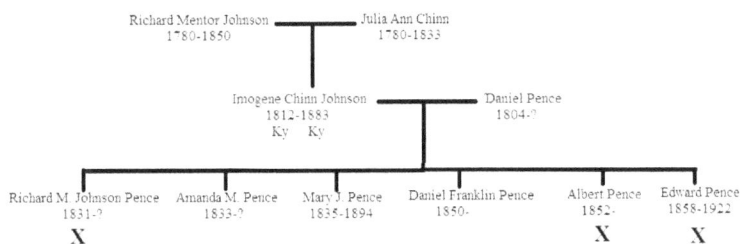

Figure 3. Descendants of Richard M. Johnson Through Imogene Johnson

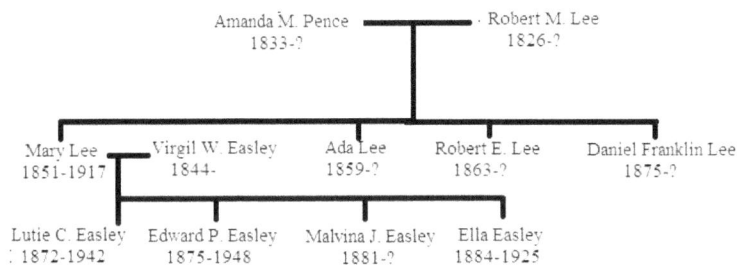

Figure 4. Descendants of Amanda Pence

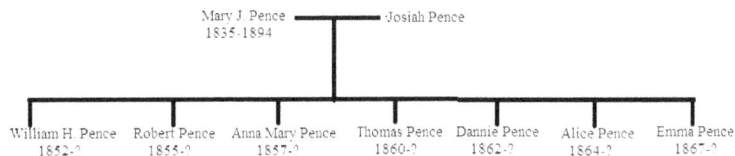

Figure 5. Descendants of Mary J. Pence

156

Daniel Franklin Pence
1850-?

Ella D.

Gracie Maria Pence
1884-?

Claude Jackson

James F. Jackson
1904-?

John Breckinridge Jackson
1908-?

Edward H. Pence
1888-?

Imogene Jackson
1910-?

Claude-Anna Jackson
1913-?

Laura Imogene Pence
1893-?

William Collis Pence
1885-?

Hattie Durham

Sarah Ella Pence
1914-?

Frank Durham Pence
1918-?

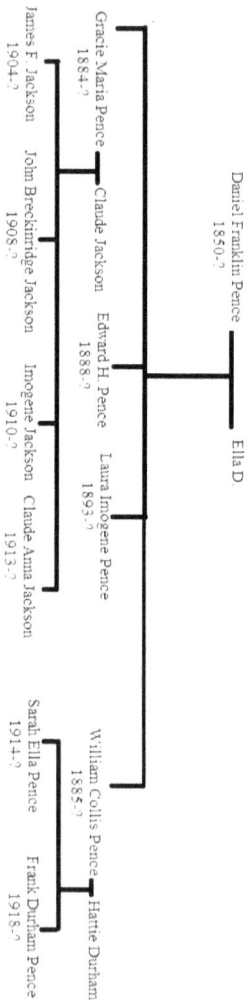

Figure 6. Descendants of Daniel F. Pence

BIBLIOGRAPHY

Biskin, Miriam. 1964. "History's Lovely Phantom." *Negro Digest* (February): 17-21.

Byrdsall, Fitzewilliam. 1842. *The History of the LocoFoco or Equal Rights Party*. New York.

DeBlack, Thomas A. 2002. "A Model Man of Chicot County: Lycurgus Johnson and Social Change." In *Southern Elite & Social Change*. Fayetville: University of Arkansas Press, 16-34.

Evans, Howard Ensign. 1197. *The Natural History of the Long Expedition to the Rocky Mountains 1819–1820*. New York: Oxford University Press.

Ewing, W.L.D. 1920. "The Visit to Springfield of Richard Mentor Johnson May 18-20, 1843." *Journal of the Illinois State Historical Society* 13 (2) (July): 192-209.

Haynes, Stan M. 2012. *The First American Political Conventions 1832–1872*. New York: McFarland.

Langworthy, Asahel. 1843. *A Biographical Sketch of Col. Richard Mentor Johnson of Kentucky*. New York: Saxton and Miles.

Lossing, Benjamin J. 2003. *Pictorial Field Book of the War of 1812*.

Mercieca, Jennifer. 2010. *Founding Fictions*. Birmingham: University of Alabama Press.

Padgett, James A. 1940. "The Letters of Colonel Richard M. Johnson of Kentucky." *Register of Kentucky State Historical Society* 38 (124) (July): 186-201.

Padgett, James A. 1941. "The Letters of Colonel Richard M. Johnson of Kentucky." *Register of Kentucky State Historical Society* 39 (129) (October): 358-367.

Schmalenberger, Sarah. 2008. "Shaping Uplift Through the Music." *Black Music Research Journal* 28 (2) (Fall): 57-83.

Scroggins, William G. 2009. *Leaves of a Stunted Shrub*, vol. 2. Nativa LLC.

Skeen, Carl Edward. 2003. *1816: America Rising*. Louisville: University of Kentucky Press.

Smith, Sydney K. 1890. *The Life, Army Record, and Public Services of D. Howard Smith*. Gilbert Company.

Thomas, R. 1837. *The Glory of America: Comprising Memoirs of the Lives and Glorious Exploits of Some of the Distinguished Officers Engaged in the Late War with Great Britain*. New York: Ezra Strong Pub.

Townsend, William. 1955. *Lincoln and the Bluegrass*. Louisville: University of Kentucky Press.

Tracey, E.C. 1845. *Memoir of the Life of Jeremiah Evarts*. Sacramento: University of California Libraries.

Trowbridge, John M. 2006. "'We Are All Slaughtered Men': The Battle of Blue Licks." *Kentucky Ancestors: Genealogical Quarterly of the Kentucky Historical Society* (Winter 2006): 58-73.

Turner, William Hobart. 1985. *Blacks in Appalachia*. Louisville: University Press of Kentucky.

Watson, Elmo Scott. 1923. "Tales of the Old Frontier." *The Warren Tribune*, November 30, 1923.

Widmer, Ted. 2005. *Martin Van Buren*. New York: MacMillan.

Wyatt-Brown, Bertram. 1970. "The Antimission Movement in the Jacksonian South: A Study in Regional Folk Culture." *The Journal of Southern History* 36 (4) (November): 501-529.

Wyatt-Brown, Bertram. 1971. "Prelude to Abolitionism: Sabbatarian Politics and the Rise of the Second Party System." *The Journal of American History* 58 (2) (September): 316-341.

Young, Bennett H. 1903. *The Battle of the Thames in Which Kentuckians Defeated the British, French, and Indians*. Louisville: J.P. Morton and Co..

1855. "Correspondences." *The Crayon* (1) (9) (February): 136-138.

1895. "By His Hand the Chief Tecumseh Fell." *The New York Times*, August 13.

2003–2004. "The US Vice President With Two Black Children." *The Journal of Blacks in Higher Education* (42) (Winter): 128.

1882. *The History of Linn County, Missouri: An Encyclopedia of Useful Information.* Birdsall & Dean.

NOTES

1 Leyland Meyer produced a doctoral dissertation on Johnson in 1932, which though largely unavailable to the public, became the basis for most later articles and works on the Vice President.

2 "Col. Richard M. Johnson: Eulogy by Hon J. C. Mather," in *The United States Democratic Review*, vol. 28 (154) (April 1851), 381.

3 Anderson Chennault Quisenberry, *Revolutionary Soldiers in Kentucky* (Baltimore: Southern Book Company, 1895), 74-75.

4 Simon Bird as mentioned in R.E. Banta, *The Ohio* (Louisville: University Press of Kentucky, 1998), 157.

5 John Filson, *The Discovery, Settlement, and Present State of Kentucke*.

6 "Some Reminiscences from the life of Col. Cave Johnson," *The Boone County Recorder* (February 1, 1877 and February 8, 1877).

7 *Louisville Journal* (October 14, 1840).

8 The average slave owner in Kentucky around 1850 possessed five slaves, half of the number owned in the Deep South. See James Ramage, *Kentucky Rising: Democracy, Slavery, and Culture from the Early Republic to the Civil War* (Louisville: University Press of Kentucky, 2011), 237.

9 William Emmons, *Authentic Biography of Colonel Johnson* (New York: Henry Mason, 1833), 7.

10 Occasionally Bryan Station is referred to as Bryant Station or Bryant's Station, though the first is the most accepted form.

11 See Banta, 165 for a description of the fort.

12 Reuben T. Durrett, *Bryant's Station and the Memorial Proceedings* (Louisville: J.P. Morton), 42.

13 Other sources, most notably H. Addington Bruce, *Daniel Boone and the Wilderness Road* (New York: MacMillan Company, 1910), 269, argue that the idea originated with Jemima Johnson herself.

14 Karl Raitz, *Kentucky's Frontier Highway: Historical Landscape along the Maysville Road* (Louisville:University Press of Kentucky, 2012), 129.

15 Elmo Scott Watson, "Tales of the Old Frontier," The Warren Tribune, November 30, 1923.

16 Pension Application of John Hawkins Craig, W6759 (January 7, 1833).

17 Letter, Robert Johnson to James Madison (September 23, 1786).

18 Letter, Robert Johnson to George Washington (August 22, 1789).

19 Ibid.

20 Letter, Robert Johnson to Beverley Randolph (August 22, 1789).

21 Letter, Henry Knox to Robert Johnson (April 13, 1790).

22 Letter, Josiah Harmar to Unknown (November 29, 1790).

23 Letters, William Simmons to Robert Johnson (September 1, 1797), (December 29, 1797), (April 6, 1798), (May 4, 1798).

24 This situation bears many similarities to the causes behind the eruption of Bacon's Rebellion a century before.

25 Letter, Robert Johnson to James Madison (September 23, 1786).

26 See Letter from Robert Johnson to James Madison (December 5, 1802) for a discussion of the upcoming election of 1804.

27 Asahel Langworthy, *A Biographical Sketch of Col. Richard Mentor Johnson of Kentucky* (New York: Saxton & Miles, 1843), 7.

28 W. H. Venable, *Beginnings of Literary Culture in the Ohio Valley* (Cincinnati: Robert Clarke and Company, 1891), 170.

29 Emmons, 9 and Benjamin Perley Poore, *Reminiscences of Sixty Years in the National Metropolis*, vol. 1 (Philadelphia: Hubbard Brothers, 1886), 153.

30 Richard M. Johnson, "Speech on the Abolition of Debt Imprisonment" (January 14, 1832).

31 Emmons, 17-18.

32 Letter, Robert Johnson to James Madison (December 5, 1802).

33 Letter, Robert Johnson to Richard Livingston (December 17, 1802).

34 Langworthy, 8.

35 Ibid., 6.

36 Annals of Congress, 16th Congress, 1st Session, 255.

37 Langworthy, 9.

38 Letter, James Johnson to Henry Clay (January 28, 1809) in James F. Hopkins, ed., The Papers of Henry Clay 1797–1814, vol. I (Louisville: University of Kentucky Press, 1959), 401.

39 *Vermont Watchman and State Journal* (August 3, 1840).

40 Letter, Robert Johnson to James Madison (December 5, 1802).

41 Henry Adams, *History of the United States,* vol. 5, (New York: Cambridge Press, 2011), 122.

42 *The Truth Seeker* (July 1, 1899) as recounted by Johnson to Francis O. J. Smith on April 10, 1834.

43 John Morrison, *An Oration Delivered in Tammany Hall: In Commemoration of the Birthday of Thomas Paine* (Evans & Brooks, 1832), 29.

44 Steven P. Brown, J*ohn McKinley and the Antebellum Supreme Court* (Montgomery: University of Alabama Press, 2012), 24-26.

45 *The Spirit of Democracy* (November 27, 1850).

46 Letter, George Eve to James Madison (November 24, 1807).

47 Mary Ellen Rowe, *Bulwark of the Republic: The American Militia in the Antebellum West* (Santa Barbara: Greenwood Publishing, 2003), 15.

48 Weymouth Jordan, *George Washington Campbell of Tennessee* (St. Petersburg: Florida State University Press, 1955), 71.

49 Langworhty, 12.

50 Letter. Richard Mentor Johnson to Thomas Jefferson (February 27, 1808).

51 Johnson Speech Before the House (January 22, 1811).

52 Ibid.

53 Ibid.

54 Ibid.

55 Ibid.

56 Banta, 167.

57 Letter, Richard Mentor Johnson to Adam Beatty (March 25, 1808), courtesy of the Filson Historical Society.

58 *Niles' Register*, vol. 2 (Baltimore: Franklin Press, 1812), 28.

59 Ibid., Supplement, 24.

60 Letter, Richard Mentor Johnson to James Madison (July 28, 1808).

61 Jordan, 78.

62 Richard Mentor Johnson (October 25, 1813).

63 Charles William Hackensmith, "Ohio Valley Higher Education in the Nineteenth Century," *Bureau of School Services: University of Kentucky* XLV (3) (March 1973): 22.

64 *Niles' Register*, vol. 2, 251.

65 Letter, Richard Mentor Johnson to James Madison (July 24, 1812).

66 Letter, Robert Johnson to James Madison (September 3, 1812).

67 Ibid.

68 Letter, Sgt. W. K. Jordan to His Wife (October 12, 1812) in *Messages and Letters of William Henry Harrison*, vol. 2 (Indiana Historical Collection, 1922), 165.

69 Letter, Daniel Curtis to Cullen Colburn Witherell (September 21, 1812) in "Indiana Magazine of History," vol. 44 (4) (December 1948), 409-418.

70 Letter, Richard Mentor Johnson to James Madison (September 18, 1812).

71 Richard Mentor Johnson before Congress on January 21, 1813 as quoted in Quentin Scott King, *Henry Clay and the War of 1812* (New York: McFaland, 2014), 105.

72 Ibid.

73   Ibid.

74   Letter, Richard Mentor Johnson to James Madison (December 10, 1812).

75   Letter, Henry Clay to James Monroe (December 23, 1812).

76   Gilpin, *The War of 1812 in the Old Northwest*, 200.

77   Commentators for years questioned the ethics of Johnson and other Congressmen for drawing two salaries by serving in both the House and the Army. *The North Carolina Standard* (January 6, 1847).

78   Benjamin Lossing, *Pictorial Field Book of the War of 1812* (New York: Harper Brothers, 1868), 200.

79   Handbill contained with Letter, Richard Mentor Johnson to John Armstrong (May 12, 1813) RG 107 (Records of the Office of the Secretary of War), Letters Received (Main Series), 1801–1870 (ARC 628093), File: J-176(7)-1813 (enclosure), NARA Microfilm Pub #M221, Roll #54.

80   Bennett H. Young, *The Battle of the Thames in Which Kentuckians Defeated the British, French, and Indians* (Louisville: J.P. Morton and Co., 1903), 64.

81   Letter, Richard Mentor Johnson to Thomas Jefferson (February 9, 1813).

82   Langworthy, 17.

83   Lossing, 495.

84   Letter, Richard Mentor Johnson to James Madison (September 18, 1812).

85   Letter, Richard Mentor Johnson to Thomas Jefferson (February 9, 1813).

86   Letter, Robert Johnson to James Madison (September 3, 1812).

87   Letter, Richard Mentor Johnson to William Henry Harrison (July 9, 1813).

88   Letter, Richard Mentor Johnson to James Madison (July 14, 1813).

89   Letter, William Henry Harrison to John Armstrong (July 23, 1813).

90   Letter, Richard Mentor Johnson to James Madison (August 9, 1813).

91   Young, 50.

92   W.L.D. Ewing, "The Visit to Springfield of Richard Mentor Johnson May 18–20, 1843," *Journal of the Illinois State Historical Society* 13 (2) (July 1920): 202.

93   Robert McElroy, *Kentucky in the Nation's History* (New York: Moffat, Yard and Company, 1909), 349.

94   *The North Carolina Standard* (May 19, 1836).

95   Ibid.

96   McElroy, 351.

97   *The North Carolina Standard* (May 19, 1836).

98   Letter, Richard Mentor Johnson to John Armstrong (December 22, 1834) in John Armstrong Jr., *Notices of the War of 1812*, vol. I (New York: William and Putnam, 1836), 234.

99   *The North Carolina Standard* (May 19, 1836).

100   Z.F. Smith, *School History of Kentucky* (Louisville: Courier Journal, 1889), 145.

101   Recounted by Richard Mentor Johnson, Ewing, 203.

102   Ibid., 204.

103   Langworthy, 22.

104   James B. Finley, *Life Among the Indians, or, Personal Reminiscences and Historical Incidents* (Cincinnati: Hitchcock and Walden, 1857), 226.

105   Langworthy, 25.

106   Pierre Benton, *Flames Across the Border 1813–1814* (Toronto: Doubleday Canada, 2011), 203.

107   *The North Carolina Standard* (May 19, 1836).

108   *Indiana State Sentinel* (December 5, 1850).

109   Letter, Richard Rush to Jared Ingersoll (October 20, 1813).

110   Thomas E. Pickett, "Presenting the Theory of Paul B. DuChaillu: Quest for a Lost Race," in *Read before the Filson Club on October 1, 1906* (Louisville: John P Morton & Company, 1907), 193

111   Edward Ellis, *The Life and Times of Col. Daniel Boone* (Philadelphia: Porter & Coates, 1884), 262.

112   John Sugden, *Tecumseh's Last Stand* (Tulsa: University of Oklahoma Press, 1990), 170.

113   *Niles' Register*, vol. 56 (Baltimore: Franklin Press, 1839), 355-356.

114   Benjamin Drake, *Life of Tecumseh, and His Brother the Prophet* (Cincinnati: E. Morgan & Co., 1841), 199-219, for a complete discussion of contemporary views on the fate of Tecumseh.

115   Letter, Terrance Kirby to Abraham Lincoln from William Townsend, *Lincoln and the Bluegrass* (Louisville: University of Ky Press, 1955), 337.

116   "Kentucky's War of 1812: The Burgoyne Cannon," *Kentucky Historical Society.* http://history.ky.gov/pdf/CommunityServices/LM58BurgoyneCannon.pdf.

117   Letter, William H. Harrison to James Madison (October 5, 1813) in *Niles' Register*, vol. 5 (Baltimore: Franklin Press, 1814), 130.

118   Langworthy, 28.

119   James F. Hopkins, ed., *The Papers of Henry Clay 1797–1814*, vol. I (Louisville: University of Kentucky Press, 1959), 740.

120   *Democratic Standard* (September 17, 1840).

121   *Kentucky Reporter* (January 1, 1814).

122   R. Thomas, *The Glory of America: Comprising Memoirs of the Lives and Glorious Exploits of Some of the Distinguished Officers Engaged in the Late War with Great Britain* (New York: Ezra Strong Pub., 1837), 157.

123 *Niles' Register*, vol. 7 (Baltimore: Franklin Press, 1815), 46.

124 Letter, William Jones to Richard Mentor Johnson (October 3, 1814).

125 Letter, Richard Mentor Johnson to James Madison (June 4, 1815).

126 Letter, Richard Mentor Johnson to James Madison (June 12, 1815).

127 Letter, James Johnson to James Madison (June 4, 1815) and Letter, James Johnson to Andrew Jackson (April 17, 1816).

128 Letter, Richard Mentor Johnson to James Madison (June 12, 1815).

129 *Daily National Intelligencer* (September 17, 1816).

130 *Niles' Register*, vol. 22 (Baltimore: Franklin Press, 1822), 59.

131 *Niles' Register*, vol. 10 (Baltimore: Franklin Press, 1816), 15.

132 *Niles' Register*, vol. 16 (Baltimore: Franklin Press, 1819), 184.

133 *Journal of the House of Representatives at the First Session of the 14th Congress* (Washington: William A. Davis, 1815), 686.

134 Letter, Richard Mentor Johnson to Thomas Jefferson (February 27, 1808).

135 Langworthy, 33.

136 Thomas, 157.

137 *Niles' Register*, vol. 12 (Baltimore: Franklin Press, 1817), 60.

138 Letter, Richard Rush to Richard Mentor Johnson (March 19, 1817) in *Niles' Register*, vol. 12 (Baltimore: Franklin Press, 1817), 174.

139 Ibid.

140 Letter, James Taylor to James Madison (January 31, 1813).

141 Letter, Richard Mentor Johnson to James Madison (January 1813).

142 *Niles' Register*, vol. 13 (Baltimore: Franklin Press, 1818), 294.

143 Ibid.

144 Carl Edward Skeen, *1816: America Rising* (Louisville: University of Kentucky Press, 2011), 80.

145 Ibid.

146 *Annals of Congress*, 14th Congress, 1st Session, 1127.

147 *Federal Republican* (June 17, 1816).

148 *Country Courier* (July 11, 1816).

149 Speech of Richard Mentor Johnson before Congress on December 4, 1816, as recorded in Col. Bennet H. Young, *Kentucky Eloquence: Past and Present* (Louisville: Ben LeBree Pub., 1907), 218.

150 Langworthy, 35.

151 Letter, Richard M. Johnson to James Taylor V (July 25, 1816), Richard M. Johnson Papers, 1816–1838, 97SC57, Library Special Collections and Archives,

Kentucky Historical Society, Frankfort.

152 *Annals of Congress*, 14th Congress, 2nd Session, 242.

153 Speech of Richard Mentor Johnson before Congress on December 4, 1816, as recorded in Col. Bennet H. Young, *Kentucky Eloquence: Past and Present* (Louisville: Ben LeBree Pub., 1907), 219.

154 Committee Report of Richard Mentor Johnson delivered before the 2nd Session of the 19th Congress (January 11, 1827).

155 Hiram Martin Chittenden, *The American Fur Trade of the Far West*, vol. 2 (University of Nebraska Press, 1986), 560.

156 *Kentucky Gazette* (October 8, 1819).

157 *American State Papers* Part 5, Volume 2: 16th Congress, 2nd Session (Gales and Seaton, 1834), 324-325.

158 Letter, John C. Calhoun to James Monroe (July 14, 1820).

159 John Fabian Witt, *Lincoln's Code: The Laws of War in American History* (New York: Simon and Schuster, 2013), 100-101.

160 Johnson and several other Senators saw the loss of a claim to Texas to not be worth the addition of Florida.

161 Witt, 103.

162 *Democratic Standard* (September 17, 1840).

163 Philip Pendleton Barbour before the House of Representatives (March 1818).

164 *The North Carolina Standard* (October 27, 1836).

165 *Niles' Register*, vol. 61 (Baltimore: Franklin Press, 1841), 136.

166 Letter, Henry Clay to Langdon Cheves (January 18, 1821).

167 Letter, Henry Clay to Langdon Cheves (June 14, 1821).

168 Letter, Henry Clay to Nicholas Biddle (September 4, 1823).

169 Thomas A. DeBlack, *Southern Elite and Social Change* (Little Rock: University of Arkansas Press), 18-19.

170 Richard M. Johnson, "Speech on the Abolition of Debt Imprisonment" (January 14, 1823).

171 2 Kings 4.

172 Letter, James Madison to Richard Mentor Johnson (April 2, 1824).

173 B. St. J. Fry, "Captain John Cleves Symmes," *The Ladies' Repository* 8 (2) (August 1871): 133-136.

174 *Niles' Register*, vol. 21 (Baltimore: Franklin Press, 1822), 241 and *Annals of Congress*, Senate, 17th Congress, 1st Session, 68-92.

175 Letter, Richard Mentor Johnson to Henry Clay (April 1, 1822).

176 *The Woodstock Age* (August 22, 1844).

177 *Burlington Free Press* (August 24, 1838).

178 Letter, Richard H. Chinn to Henry Clay (September 10, 1828).

179 Letter, John Chambers to John J. Crittenden (1829), *The Life of John J. Crittenden*, vol. 1-2 (New York: J.B. Lippincott and Company, 1873), 79.

180 Letter, Worden Pope to Andrew Jackson (May 1829), *The Papers of Andrew Jackson* (Nashville: University of Tennessee Press, 2007), 256.

181 Speech of Richard M. Johnson as contained in "Col. Richard M. Johnson. Eulogy by Hon J. C. Mather," in *The United States Democratic Review* vol. 28 (154) (April 1851), 378.

182 Langworthy, 40 and Robert Richardson, *Memoirs of Alexander Campbell*, vol. 1Philadelphia: J.B. Lippincott, 1870), 536.

183 Wayne E. Fuller, *Morality and the Mail in 19th Century America* (Chicago: University of Illinois Press, 2003), 27-38 and Richardson, 536.

184 Richard Mentor Johnson, "Speech on Sunday Mail Delivery" (January 19, 1829).

185 Tracy, *Memoir of Evarts*, 363.

186 Morrison, 29.

187 Ibid., 23.

188 John Thomas Brown, *Churches of Christ: A Historical, Biographical, and Pictorial History of Churches of Christ in the United States, Australasia, England and Canada* (New York: J.P. Morton, 1904), 429.

189 Letter, Henry Clay to Richard Mentor Johnson (April 12, 1822).

190 *Maysville Eagle* (June 8, 1830).

191 Letter, Leslie Combs to Nicholas Biddle (July 27, 1835).

192 *Kentucky Gazette* (April 2, 1836).

193 *Rutland Herald* (March 24, 1840).

194 *Congressional Globe*, House of Representatives, 24th Congress, 1st Session, 378.

195 Letter, Lewis Cass to Richard M. Johnson (April 16, 1836) in *Congressional Globe*, House of Representatives, 24th Congress, 1st Session, 295.

196 *Congressional Globe*, House of Representatives, 24th Congress, 1st Session, 295.

197 Ibid.

198 *Congressional Globe*, Senate, 24th Congress, 1st Session, 136-137.

199 Speech of Richard Mentor Johnson before Congress on December 4, 1816, as recorded in Col. Bennet H. Young, *Kentucky Eloquence: Past and Present* (Louisville: Ben LeBree Pub., 1907), 220.

200 *The Caledonian* (December 12, 1837).

201 Albert J. Beveridge, *The Life of John Marshall*, vol. 4 (New York: Houghton

Mifflin, 1919), 950.

202 *Annals of Congress*, 16th Congress, 1st Session, 355.

203 Ibid., 353-354.

204 William Hobart Turner, *Blacks in Appalachia* (Louisville: University Press of Kentucky, 1985), 77.

205 George D. Prentice, *Louisville Journal* (July 8, 1835).

206 C. W. Webber, *Historical and Revolutionary Incidents of the Early Settlers of the United States* (Philadelphia: Quaker City Publishing, 1867), 377.

207 *Vermont Watchman* (December 13, 1836).

208 There was possibly a son who did not survive as well who is mentioned by Margaret Bayard Smith in *The First 40 Years of Washington Society* (New York: Charles Scribners & Sons, 1906), 206.

209 Turner, 76.

210 See the Appendix for a detailed genealogy of the Johnson Family.

211 *The Lexington Observer & Kentucky Reporter* (November 29, 1832).

212 George D. Prentice, *Louisville Journal* (July 8, 1835).

213 Only Connecticut, New Hampshire, Vermont, New Jersey, and New York did not have laws on the books at this time. The term mulatto, while traditionally implying half white-half black, could sometimes be stretched depending upon the nature of the jury or legislature.

214 Letter, Margaret Bayard Smith to Mrs. Boyd (January 12, 1827) in *The First 40 Years of Washington Society* (New York: Charles Scribners & Sons, 1906), 206-207.

215 Letter, Margaret Bayard Smith to Mrs. Kirkpatrick (1824) Ibid., 166.

216 *Vermont Watchman* (December 13, 1836).

217 *Louisville Journal* (July 14, 1835).

218 Letter, Amos Kendall to Martin Van Buren (August 22, 1839). Kendall was Postmaster General under Jackson and Van Buren and had gotten his start as a newspaper writer and editor at a Johnson owned paper in Kentucky.

219 Henry Highland Garnet, "The Past and the Present Condition, and the Destiny of the Colored Race" (1848), 24.

220 *Green-Mountain Freeman* (June 20, 1845).

221 A 50-year-old mulatto named Patience Chine is in fact still listed as living in Frankfort, Ky in the 1860 census.

222 Sarah Schmalenberger, "Shaping Uplift Through the Music," *Black Music Research Journal* 28 (2) (Fall 2008): 60.

223 *Albany Argus* (March 23, 1831).

224 Lincoln-Douglas Debates (1858).

225 Miles Smith, "Turning Up Their Noses at the Colonel: Eastern Aristocracy, Western Democracy, and Richard Mentor Johnson," *Register of the Kentucky Historical Society* 111 (4) (Autumn 2013): 525-561.

226 Charles Wiltse, *John C. Calhoun*, vol. 2 (New York: Bobs Merrill, 1968), 37.

227 John F. Marszalek, *The Petticoat Affair: Manners, Mutiny, and Sex in Andrew Jackson's White House* (Baton Rouge:LSU Press, 2000), 116.

228 Letter, John Norvell to John McLean (January 23, 1832) as quoted in Meyer, 398.

229 Ely Moore, "Tribute to Col. Richard M. Johnson," Speech at Masonic Hall, New York (March 13, 1833).

230 Duff Green, *Political Register* (April 1833).

231 Adam Jortner, *The Gods of Prophetstown* (Oxford: Oxford University Press, 2012), 216.

232 Richard Emmons, *Tecumseh, or the Battle of the Thames* (New York: Elton & Harrison, 1836), 9.

233 Robert V. Remini, *Jackson and the Course of American Democracy* (New York: Harper and Collins, 1984), 252-253.

234 Martin Van Buren, *Autobiography of Martin Van Buren*, vol. 2 (Washington: US Government Printing Office, 1920), 744-745.

235 Niven, *Martin Van Buren*, 396 and Robert Bolt, "Vice President Richard M. Johnson of Kentucky: Hero of the Thames—Or the Great Amalgamator?," *Register of the Kentucky Historical Society* 75 (July 1977): 201.

236 Francis Preston Blair, *The Extra Globe for 1835* (Washington: Blair and Rives, 1835), 8.

237 Letter, John Catron to Andrew Jackson (March 21, 1835).

238 Register of the Kentucky Historical Society, vol. 106 (KHS, 2008), 385.

239 *Niles Weekly Register*, vol. 48 (Baltimore: Franklin Press, 1835), 246.

240 *Burlington Free Press* (December 30, 1836).

241 Acceptance Speech of Richard Mentor Johnson (May 23, 1835) in *Niles' Register*, vol. 48 (Baltimore: Franklin Press, 1835), 329-330.

242 *Burlington Free Press* (August 12, 1836).

243 *State Journal* (August 23, 1836).

244 *Vermont Watchman* (December 13, 1836).

245 Ibid.

246 *Green Mountain Freeman* (June 20, 1845).

247 Marc Leepson, *What So Proudly We Hailed: Francis Scott Key, A Life* (New York: Macmillan, 2014), 180.

248 *Burlington Free Press* (September 16, 1836).

249 *State Journal* (May 24, 1836).

250 *State Journal* (August 30, 1836).

251 *Burlington Free Press* (July 8, 1836).

252 *Rutland Herald* (December 20, 1836).

253 Blair, 16.

254 *Niles' Register*, vol. 51 (Baltimore: Franklin Press, 1836), 151.

255 *Burlington Free Press* (December 30, 1836).

256 *The North Carolina Standard* (September 22, 1836).

257 *Constantine Republican* (October 12, 1836).

258 Thomas Pinckney of SC in 1800, Elbridge Gerry of Massachusetts in 1812, and John C. Calhoun of SC in 1824.

259 *The North Carolina Standard* (December 14, 1836).

260 *Vermont Watchman* (December 13, 1836).

261 From Johnson's Inaugural Address to Congress from the *Constantine Republican* (March 29, 1837).

262 *Vermont Watchman and State Journal* (March 21, 1837).

263 *Maumee Express* (December 30, 1837.)

264 *The North Carolina Standard* (July 19, 1837) and *Western Courier* (July 20, 1837).

265 *The Somerset Herald and Farmers' and Mechanics'Register* (December 16, 1845).

266 *Maumee Express* (July 29, 1837).

267 *New York Tribune* (October 2, 1841).

268 *Vermont Watchman and State Journal* (December 4, 1837).

269 *Indiana State Sentinel* (February 14, 1849).

270 *Kentucky Gazette*, (March 14, 1839).

271 McElroy, 558.

272 Bertram Wyatt-Brown, "The Antimission Movement in the Jacksonian South: A Study in Regional Folk Culture," *The Journal of Southern History* 36 (4) (November 1970): 523.

273 Richard Mentor Johnson as recorded in the *Illinois Free Trader* (May 23, 1840).

274 John Wilson Townsend, *Richard Hickman Menefee* (Boston: Neale Publishing, 1907), 249.

275 *The Lancaster Gazette* (November 8, 1850).

276 *Vermont Watchman and State Journal* (April 18, 1842).

277 Letter, Amos Kendall to Martin van Buren (August 22, 1839).

278 Ibid.

279 Harriet Martineau, *Retrospect of Western Travel* (Los Angeles: Applewood Books, 2007), 155.

280 *Maumee Express* (April 28, 1838).

281 *Niles' Register,* vol. 13 (Baltimore: Franklin Press, 1817), 4.

282 Letter, Thomas L. McKenney to Richard Mentor Johnson (June 27, 1820) in *Niles' Register*, vol. 16 (Baltimore: Franklin Press, 1820), 94.

283 Ibid.

284 Angie Debo, *The Rise and Fall of the Choctaw Republic* (Tulsa: University of Oklahoma Press, 1967), 44.

285 Letter, Richard Mentor Johnson to James Barbour (September 27, 1825).

286 Roger G. Kennedy, *Cotton and Conquest: How the Plantation System Acquired Texas* (Tulsa: University of Oklahoma Press, 2013), 304.

287 Carolyn Thomas Foreman, *Chronicles of Oklahoma* 6 (4) (December 1928): 458.

288 Letter, Robert Ould to Peter B. Porter (July 16, 1838) in Carolyn Thomas Foreman, "The Choctaw Academy," *Chronicles of Oklahoma* 9 (4) (December 1931): 384-385.

289 *Cherokee Phoenix* (August 6, 1828).

290 *Vermont Phoenix* (July 19, 1839).

291 *Vermont Watchman and State Journal* (August 28, 1837).

292 *True American* (September 8, 1838).

293 Letter, Andrew Jackson to Francis P. Blair (February 15, 1840).

294 Letter, Richard Mentor Johnson to a Friend (June 8, 1839), in *Niles' Register*, vol. 56 (Baltimore: Franklin Press, 1839), 275.

295 *Maumee City Express* (May 25, 1839).

296 *Maumee City Express* (March 16, 1839).

297 *The Ohio Democrat and Dover Advertiser* (May 22, 1840).

298 *Rutland Herald* (May 26, 1840).

299 Ibid.

300 *The Caledonian* (May 26, 1840) and *The North Carolina Standard* (June 10, 1840).

301 *Vermont Watchman and State Journal* (August 3, 1840).

302 *The Columbia Democrat* (December 21, 1839).

303 *Burlington Free Press* (April 10, 1840).

304 *Boon's Lick Times* (March 28, 1840).

305 *Burlington Free Press* (December 14, 1838).

306 Kevin C. Julius, *The Abolitionist Decade 1829-1838* (New York: McFarland, 2004), 232.

307 *Maumee City Express* (August 10, 1839).

308 *The Caledonian* (August 6, 1839).

309 *The Voice of Freedom* (August 31, 1839).

310 *The North Carolina Standard* (January 29, 1840).

311 *Green-Mountain Freeman* (June 20, 1845).

312 Letter, Robert Perkins Letcher to John Crittenden (June 14, 1840) in reference to Polk's failure to use Johnson in Tennessee.

313 Letter, John C. Calhoun to Armistead Hurt (November 2, 1840).

314 Poe was known to have published stories in Whig journals such as *The American Whig Review* and sought jobs with the Harrison and Tyler administrations, and thus would have not attacked Scott a fellow Whig.

315 Edgar Allen Poe, *The Man That Was Used Up*.

316 Ibid.

317 *The North Carolina Standard* (June 17, 1840).

318 *The North Carolina Standard* (July 15, 1840).

319 Ibid.

320 *Vermont Watchman and State Journal* (December 2, 1839).

321 Ted Widmer, *Martin Van Buren* (New York: MacMillan, 2005), 138.

322 *The Caledonian* (December 31, 1839).

323 *The Pilot and Transcript* (June 23, 1840).

324 *Democratic Standard* (August 20, 1840).

325 *Vermont Telegraph* (March 10, 1841).

326 *Rutland Herald* (March 23, 1841).

327 *The North Carolina Standard* (March 24, 1841).

328 Fitzwilliam Byrdsall, *The History of the LocoFoco or Equal Rights Party* (New York: 1842), 13-20.

329 Letter, John C. Easton to James D. Easton (May 1, 1844).

330 Letter, Robert Perkins Letcher to John J. Crittenden (February 24, 1842) in *The Life of John J. Crittenden*, vol. 1-2 (Boston: J.B. Lippincott and Company, 1873), 172.

331 Letter, Robert Perkins Letcher to John J. Crittenden (February 25, 1842) in *The Life of John J. Crittenden*, vol. 1-2 (Boston: J.B. Lippincott and Company, 1873), 171.

332 Letter, Robert Perkins Letcher to John J. Crittenden (February 26, 1842) in *The Life of John J. Crittenden*, vol. 1-2 (Boston: J.B. Lippincott and Company,

1873), 172.

333 Letter, Robert Perkins Letcher to John Crittenden (June 2, 1842) in *The Life of John J. Crittenden*, vol. 1-2 (Boston: J.B. Lippincott and Company, 1873), 181.

334 Letter, John C. Calhoun to Thomas G. Clemson (January 23, 1842) and Letter, John C. Calhoun to James H. Hammond (September 10, 1842).

335 Letter, Andrew Jackson to Martin Van Buren (September 22, 1843).

336 Letter, John J. Crittenden to R.P. Letcher (January 13, 1842) in *The Life of John J. Crittenden*, vol. 1-2 (Boston: J.B. Lippincott and Company, 1873), 197.

337 *New York Tribune* (January 17, 1842).

338 *The Ohio Democrat* (January 27, 1842).

339 *Democratic Standard* (September 30, 1840).

340 Letter, Thomas Fletcher to James K. Polk (January 28, 1842).

341 Ewing, 193.

342 *Illinois State Register* (May 24, 1843).

343 Ewing, 201.

344 Letter, Robert Perkins Letcher to John J. Crittenden (December 8, 1842) in *The Life of John J. Crittenden*, vol. 1-2 (Boston: J.B. Lippincott and Company, 1873), 195.

345 Letter, Winfield Scott to John J. Crittenden (October 14, 1843) in *The Life of John J. Crittenden*, vol. 1-2 (Boston: J.B. Lippincott and Company, 1873), 203-204.

346 Letter, John C. Calhoun to James Edward Calhoun (February 7, 1844).

347 Thomas Fleming, The Wages of Fame (New York: Forge Books, 1999), 389.

348 *Niles' National Register*, vol. 66 (Baltimore: Franklin Press, 1844), 93.

349 Letter, James Pinckney Henderson to Sam Houston (May 20, 1844) in Andrew Jackson Houston Papers #3473.

350 John Mack Farragher, *The Life and Legend of an American Pioneer* (New York: Holt, 1992), 354-362.

351 *Green-Mountain Freeman* (June 25, 1846).

352 *North Carolina Standard* (June 18, 1845).

353 *New York Daily Tribune* (August 21, 1846).

354 *Sunbury Academics* (June 7, 1845).

355 *Indiana State Sentinel* (August 23, 1849).

356 *New York Daily Tribune* (May 14, 1846).

357 *New York Daily Tribune* (August 21, 1846).

358 *Vermont Watchman* (March 30, 1848).

359 Letter, Richard Mentor Johnson to John C. Spencer (November 26, 1841).

360 *The Lancaster Gazette* (March 16, 1849).

361 *Louisville Daily Journal* (November 9, 1850).

362 *The North Carolina Standard* (June 5, 1850).

363 *Sunbury American* (June 15, 1850).

364 Syndey K. Smith, *The Life, Army Record, and Public Services of D. Howard Smith* (Gilbert Company, 1890), 28.

365 *New York Daily Tribune* (November 21, 1850).

366 *The Anti-slavery Bugle* (November 30, 1850).

367 "Col. Richard M. Johnson: Eulogy by Hon J. C. Mather," in *The United States Democratic Review* 28 (154) (April 1851); 376-381.

368 *Daily Globe* (December 4, 1850).

369 "Correspondences," *The Crayon* 1 (9) (February 28, 1855): 138.

370 *Danville Kentucky Tribune* (September 22, 1843).

371 *The Ohio Democrat and Dover Advertiser* (January 31, 1840).

372 Emmons, 36.

373 *The History of Linn County, Missouri: An Encyclopedia of Useful Information* (Birdsall & Dean, 1882), 560-561.